STATE OF THE SCHOOL

State of the School

Transformative strategies to activate, empower, and inspire every member of your school community while reaching your true potential as a leader - and have fun doing it.

MEGAN TRAVER

CONTENTS

ACKNOWLEDGMENTS

This book is dedicated to my mentor and friend, Dr. Kristi Kahl.

PREFACE

Before we get started on our journey together, I'd like to make sure I'm clear about something: I do not have all of the perfect answers on how to lead a school - I'm still learning and growing as an educational leader and always will be. The purpose of this book is to share about a process that I know works. I will share some of the ways of thinking and things I have done with teams of school leaders and students that have led to some *incredible* results. My hope is that you find at least one or two gold nuggets out of this book that inspire you, spark you to think about something in a new way, or even give you a few practical ideas on things you can do to take your school, team, or organization to the next level. I know this process works and I know it can work for you, too.

This book is for anyone who is leading in any way on a school site, in a district, on a team, or in any organization. Principals, assistant principals, teacher leaders, school psychologists, school counselors, office supervisors, head custodians, parents, CEOs, business owners, superintendents, directors. If you oversee any work or any kind of a team, this book is for you.

If you are a parent or friend of someone who works in education, get this book for him or her. We should all be on Team Education. As Whitney Houston says in her hit song from the 80's, "I believe the children are our future.." She's right.

Another reason I have written this book is due to the atrocity of the "achievement gap" happening in education. That is, currently, the level of academic success of a student can best be predicted based on the color of his or her skin. Ah, *a big hard no on that being allowed to happen.* We absolutely cannot allow this to continue. There is *no reason* for this pattern to be occurring other than because we have a system of education that is failing our students of color. History and current data shows for the most part, we have allowed schools that are inhabited by students of color to flail. That needs to end here and now. The strategies in this book can help you and your school and district provide the opportunity for success to all students regardless of the color of their skin.

The foundation of this work has happened within the field of education, therefore that will be the lens we will look through during the course of this book. But there are many connections that can be made to the work in any organization in terms of leadership principles. Get on in here and make those connections - they are all here for you.

You probably have many books about leadership on your bookshelves. This book is not like those books.

I humbly and graciously offer you the information and stories in this book and I hope you can receive them on any level that benefits you, your team, your clients, and the people you serve.

So, let's begin.

INTRODUCTION

I call myself and honestly, I guess I am, an "accidental principal." I had no idea I would ever end up in education, let alone end up in educational leadership. I started out as a substitute teacher to pick up some income in between traveling and my work as an event coordinator. I liked substitute teaching. I was pretty good at it, too. I got asked back a lot, which eventually turned into an interview and a job offer. I ended up turning down my first job offer because I decided to stick with event coordinating. And then 9/11 happened and so many events were postponed or canceled. By some stroke of fate or luck, the school that originally offered me the full-time job that I turned down called me to offer me a long-term substitute position. Clearly they were desperate. They really were.

I would be signing on for a job for which I did not have one credit towards a teaching credential. They needed someone to teach math and I had enough college credits in math to get an emergency credential. Now that I think of it, I was also an "accidental teacher."

I was ecstatic when I was hired...Mostly because I needed some income. And, to be honest, I quite enjoyed teaching. It seemed like a great opportunity.

The school gave me one day of prep ahead of beginning my assignment to get prepared. I will never forget the fateful words the principal at the time said to me as I looked around the barren bungalow room. She said, "I need you to raise the test scores."

"Raise the test scores? OK!" Looking back now, I realize how absolutely little I knew and understood about "the test" and test scores, let alone how to raise them. But I was a "go-getter." I didn't know what "raising the test scores" meant or how to do it, but I was ready to give my students my all.

The first class of students I would be teaching were on "overflow," which means that the families of these students enrolled their children a bit later than other families and therefore didn't fit into the regular master schedule, but the school did what they could to accommodate them. This also happened to be a class of all English language learners, some who had just recently moved to our city and some who were new to the country. All of the students were bussed in from the most impoverished areas of our city.

It was in this class that I first met Miguel. And Hugo. Two students that have impacted me forever. Miguel was feisty. Hugo was compliant. Miguel came to school almost every day with a big bag of chips and a liter of soda. Hugo dutifully ate his lunch from the cafeteria.

I adored both students, but to be honest, Miguel and I sometimes butted heads. One day a few months into my year of teaching Miguel disappeared out of nowhere. I later found out that he had been placed in foster care because his mom had been giving him $20 each week and then leaving him for the week to take care of himself and his little brother. He spent that $20 on chips and soda for himself and his brother, like a pre-teen probably would. Little did I know about the responsibilities he was dealing with at home while I was teaching him in our classroom.

Hugo excelled. He was a joy. He had parents at home who pushed him to succeed.

You learn a lot about the world of teaching when you encounter and understand the polarity of these circumstances. Miguel and Hugo are two of the reasons I know deep in my soul that we need to be the best of the best in education. There is such a wide variety of circumstances and range of challenges to face and overcome. *All our students deserve the best. All of them.* Both Hugo *and* Miguel.

On the first day of my teaching career I held up the math book and asked my students, "Ok, kids, where are you in this textbook?" They said, "We've never seen that textbook." I was speechless for a good moment. Eventually I naively asked, "Well then, what have you been doing?" They said, "We've been watching movies." (Me in my head: Huh? And my expression: Huh?) "The last one was *Armageddon*." You should have seen my face. You. Should. Have. Seen. My. Face. It was November. And school started in early September.

I had my work cut out for me.

So, all I knew to do was to teach the heck out of math. I tried to make it engaging and as "real life" focused as I could just as I would have wanted it taught to me. I used the book and took it chapter by chapter. Something I would never recommend knowing what I know now. You need to be so much more strategic than that.

But, by some wild miracle, in May my students raised their test scores on the state test. By quite a bit, too. The math coach and principal met with me at the beginning of the following school year and asked, "What did you do?" I said, "I don't know. I just taught the math."

It makes me realize that half the battle is just good teaching. (Haha - "just good teaching" as if that's easy...) But if I look back now, I know that I could have raised the test scores a whole lot more. And the students could have learned a whole lot more. I wonder now.. How many schools and teachers out there are achieving bumps in data based on good teaching but could be achieving a whole lot more?

There is a whole lot more. *A WHOLE LOT MORE.*

I taught for four years under the incredible leadership of my first principal who taught me so much about leadership by being under hers. She had high expectations and she held us accountable, but with support to meet her high expectations. She was always pushing herself, too - you could tell. And it inspired me to push myself. She was strategic and inclusive with our work. She had an ambitious vision for our school and a knack for being able to pull our efforts together. She led us to great, *great* achievements, including turning our school from almost being taken over by the state to being awarded the "Blue Ribbon Award" from the state of California in just six years. That is a huge turnaround.

One year during my years of teaching, she ran a staff meeting and called it "State of the School." I remember two department heads sharing-out data. It was math and ELA. I had turned in my math facts and integer data to the department head about a week prior - and here it was compiled into our school-wide data.

Watching this State of the School meeting was a transformative experience for me. I realized that even though I was just "doing my thing" in my classroom, it led to something greater, something bigger. My work contributed to a school-wide effort.

The title "State of the School" is so meaningful. I remember watching the "State of the Union" as my parents somewhat forced me to do when I was a kid. It's where our president and most of our elected democracy come together to talk about what's going on in our country.

How is the state of our union? What has gone on so far? What is next? And what are our priorities going forward?

I didn't realize at the time how much that early morning staff meeting was going to impact me and drive my leadership vision for the rest of my career. I just took in the experience and reflected on what it meant. I saw that our collective effort was greater than the sum of our parts. In short, I saw that everybody on the team was absolutely critical to the success of the organization. I had no idea how life-changing that experience would be.

After five years of teaching, I was promoted into a new leadership role as a "TOSA" (teacher on special assignment) at a school that needed the support of a "math coach." A math coach in our district is someone who supports math teachers in learning and implementing the most effective teaching strategies. I served as a math coach at a school site and also part-time in the district while serving multiple sites for four years. It taught me that one of the most difficult tasks is working with adults who are resistant to change.

Frankly, kids can be a bit more adaptable than adults - kids are more naturally used to the change process since they are constantly in a state of growth as they grow from children into adults. The brains of pre-teens and teenagers are not even fully formed. Not even close.

But adult brains are likely fully formed. Which makes it a bit frustrating sometimes because change, growth, and doing things differently than "they've always been done" can be quite hard for some adults. Yet, this work cannot be done without commitment from the adults.

The adults in education are critical - the teachers, in particular. Based on John Hattie's extensive research, the level of effectiveness of classroom instruction is the single most important factor in determining the success of a child in education. And our teachers are on the front lines of that work, which means that they must be given the best tools, best strategies, and best support possible. That's why you cannot just "throw in the towel" when it comes to working with adults. *They are too critical to this work to not fully invest in them.*

Adults in education are people with needs and feelings, too - it is not just the students. Sometimes in education we focus solely on meeting the needs of students, but in those instances, we are missing a key component to achieving school success. Adults want and need support, appreciation, and encouragement, too. And while sometimes adults can be the most resistant to change, school transformation cannot happen without them. Therefore, a part of your job is figuring out how to meet the needs of and support *all the people* on your campus or in your organization. And, yes, that is a *huge* job. More on that later.

One summer evening after four years of working as a math coach, I got a call from the district office. It was totally unexpected. "Hi Megan. You are being promoted and will now be an assistant principal." Me, "What..? Really..?" The assistant superintendent was clearly way more confident about this promotion than I was. "Are you excited?" she asked exuberantly. After a long pause, I shared, "I don't know."

I was so scared. Had they made a mistake? Me, an assistant principal?

I'm pretty sure, "I don't know" is not the best response to a promotion. But, lucky for me, that wasn't enough to derail their decision.

Every step so far for me has felt "accidental." As in, who was I to be in any of these positions?

I had a similar experience when I became a principal. The former principal at my school had been moved and a new principal had not yet been identified. The administrative school year had already begun. Teachers were asking me, as the assistant principal, questions I could not answer because I did not know. I was the assistant principal for god's sake.

Then I got another fateful call, "You are going to be the principal at your school."

I don't know if the district had many other options under the circumstances, so I think I was sort of it. Eek. I thought, "Well, ok, *let's give this a shot.*"

I was now the principal at one of the toughest, if not *the toughest*, school in our large urban district of 84 schools. 1,100 students. An abysmally low percentage of those students were meeting grade level standards at the time. Gangs, poverty, and a highly impacted neighborhood was bearing on top of the school. Several teachers and staff members have shared with me that when they found out they were placed or displaced to this school, they cried.

I don't know how to say this in a nice way, but I don't think a bunch of people were clamoring for the principalship at this particular school. Leading this school was going to be a huge undertaking as we faced a multitude of challenges. And I was a brand new principal! Haha!

Where most others saw a hopeless situation, I saw opportunity and possibility. What better place to start than at the bottom? The only place to go was up.

I had worked with these students, staff members, teachers, and parents for three years as the assistant principal and what I knew was there was so much more that everyone in this school was capable of than what the current data showed. I saw this school as a diamond in the rough. And I couldn't wait to show everyone what these amazing people, school, and community were made of.

We were all underdogs. Man, do I love an underdog. And I was going to be the accidental principal leading the way. I really had nothing to lose. Maybe it wasn't such an accident after all.

Somehow, somewhere in my mind, the idea of the "State of the School" lingered for almost ten years after that fateful early morning meeting.

On the top of my list of things to do during my first year as principal was to meet with each department head to work on setting year-long goals. These goals were going to be real - as in realistic, meaningful, and thoughtful. You know how sometimes people write goals that are sort of fake, you know, just to check off the box of "Oh yeah, I set some goals." Where someone picks a goal out of the air. For instance, a goal like: "All students will score at grade level proficiency on the state test" when only 30% of the students are coming in at grade level proficiency. Or, just as disconcerting, "30% of students will score at grade level proficiency on the state test" when that's what they came in at. I wasn't going to do that.

We set real goals. Real goals that mattered. Real goals that measured what we knew needed to be measured to monitor student achievement and well-being. Goals that were ambitious, but also realistic. Not too low, not too high. We needed to measure the right things, too. This took time and energy. Precious time and energy that was well worth it in the long run.

So, you're probably sitting here thinking, "Yeah, we write goals. But that is not necessarily impacting achievement at my school. We're trying our best. We're working so hard."

Yes, yes, you are. You are trying your best and you are working so hard.

But what if there was a way to pull the collective efforts of your whole school together to create a truly transformative effort and, therefore, impact student success?

There is. It is the State of the School. The State of the School process requires you ask yourself and be able to answer three key questions:

What is the state of the school?
How do we know?
And what do we do now?

I served as the principal at my first school for six amazing years - my first assignment as a principal. To reiterate, the school is located in one of the toughest, most impoverished, most impacted, most violent areas of Long Beach, California. We had all of the challenges. *All of the challenges.*

And yet we *triumphed.*

We achieved a level of success that almost no one thought was possible.

We met the district target growth measures in both ELA and math on the state test for three years in a row (the SBAC had only been implemented for three years at that time). We were one of only four schools in our large urban school district to do that out of 84 schools in our district - and *the only secondary school to achieve that.* And this is in a district that has been awarded the title "Best Urban School District in the Nation" from the Broad Foundation. We are a district filled with superstar leaders, teachers, students, and schools. To achieve what we achieved was almost beyond anyone's imagination.

We were doing something no other school was doing under the conditions we were doing them under. We were making gains and achieving success that were pretty much unprecedented at a school with 98% of our students on a free or reduced lunch program, an abundance of English language learners, and in an area riddled with crime, violence, and poverty. We didn't let the challenges get in our way. We were doing something magical.. Something right. Really right. Our superintendent at the time posted this on Twitter after one of our State of the School addresses:

"If all schools had the collected efficacy of this staff, *there wouldn't be an achievement gap.*" (My emphasis.)

These were some of the most inspirational, life work's-affirming words I have ever read. You could have knocked me over with a breeze when I read this Tweet. If you ask me what I dream of most deeply in my soul, it is that there is no longer an achievement gap and that all students have equal access to a top-notch education regardless of demographics. *Amen.*

We were working together and taking risks. We were looking at data and using it to inform decisions about our work and next steps. A non-profit organization that measures student achievement called WestEd identified our school as an "outlier." We were making gains that shouldn't have been possible, gains that were completely unexpected.

So, you're probably wondering.. How did we do it?

I know how we did it. And I'm going to tell you so you can do it at your school and in your district or organization, too.

You are probably going to have a million questions as you read through the first chapter and twice as many excuses for why it won't work at your school or organization, with your staff, with your challenges, etc. Be patient. Read the whole book first and then take a deep breath. Read it again with an open mind and an open heart. I believe in you! You can do this!

| **1** |

Chapter 1: State of the School

WHAT IS IT AND WHY IT WORKS

"If everyone is moving forward together, then success takes care of itself." —Henry Ford

The State of the School is a year-long process. It includes three key things: a *school-wide event* called the "State of the School Address" held at two specific points during the school year; *a way of thinking* that is ambitious, optimistic, inclusive, and courageous; and *a way of working* that is strategic, laser-focused, and action-oriented.

The State of the School process is a year-long plan to strategize, implement, and achieve focused goals as a school through the expanded leadership capacity of a substantial group of leaders and stakeholders on campus in order to bring about a legitimately higher level of student achievement and success.

State of the School Address Event

So, what do these twice-yearly events look like and what are they all about?

Although the State of the School Address is sort of a culminating event, it is never, by any means, the end of the journey. These events serve as a marker. They provide us with an opportunity to stop, ask, and address these three key questions:

What is the state of the school?
How do we know?
And what do we do now?

The State of the School Addresses oftentimes feel like the best, most inspirational, and fun days of the school year...By far. During this event, you will dedicate an entire jam-packed one-hour meeting to sharing out about progress toward school-wide and department-specific goals. Leadership team members get three to four minutes each to present about their specific goals - the progress their team has made, the data they've collected, the work they are most proud of, and a plan for next steps. When done well, the State of the School meeting can be electric.

One of the most powerful parts of the State of the School Address is when other departments and sets of teachers and staff that they don't normally work with get to see and better understand what other teams are doing. I can barely describe to you the inspiration and motivation this brings to teams across the campus. This is so very important: People realize that they are not the only ones working their tails off and trying to make a difference. It helps to alleviate some of the loneliness that can potentially come from teaching and working late nights alone in a classroom. This helps your teachers and staff know they are not alone. They, instead, can see and deeply understand that they are part of a magnificent team of people doing magnificent things. Not only do teachers get to celebrate their own work, but they also get to see the awesome things that other people are doing.

The State of the School event is, hands down, one of the best, most impactful parts of this whole process. It's when your team stops everything to acknowledge how far you've come and where you are going next. It is inspiration and information all rolled into one. It's collective efficacy on steroids.

Our State of the School events didn't start out as anything that I would call "spectacular." The same good thinking was still there, though, and that mattered a lot.

Our first State of the School was a "gallery walk." Each department had created a tri-fold poster outlining their goals, progress toward their goals, data graphs, student work samples, and ideas for next steps. Similar to what is done for a gallery walk in the classroom, we broke into small groups and worked our way around the room to look at each of the posters. I provided each teacher with a reflection sheet to be turned in at the end of the meeting.

As simple as this first round of the event was, it was clear that the experience had a strong impact on the teachers. Teachers expressed a genuine and excited interest in what other departments were doing and achieving. It was also nice to have some realia we could display in the foyer of the school to share this great work with all who walked in.

It was also a joy to see each department committed to a level of excellence in terms of what they created with their posters and the information they thoughtfully selected and shared with the school. It was clear to see that they were proud of their work. And they genuinely had work they should be proud of. As a school-site leader, I was thrilled.

For the next round of the State of the School Address, I asked each department to have a representative from the department stay at the tri-fold poster in order to present to each of the small groups. Looking back now, it is easy to see how this was a critical first step that led toward an all-school presentation - but at the time I didn't know that yet. I just thought, "What if the groups had questions or wanted more information?" Then the department representative was there to go more in-depth, if necessary. It was a warm-up for what was yet to come.

Then, realizing the potential of this kind of event, this work, I knew it was time to shift to an all-school presentation. I told department heads: You are going to stand up and explain your work to the whole school. I need it to come from you and I want to make sure that everyone hears about it.

This came from me watching the work of our departments evolve into incredibly strategic and meaningful work. It was starting to reach a whole new level. Department heads were developing into very strong leaders, too. They were really starting to strategically push their teams to greater heights. And that work was paying off as shown by the data. It was time to shine a bigger and brighter light on this work.

Having teacher leaders make these presentations might be somewhat of a bigger "ask" than it seems on the surface. I have found that many people get pretty nervous presenting in front of their colleagues. And this is while they have no trouble presenting in front of thirty-five middle schoolers. There seems to be a different level of pressure and anxiety while presenting in front of colleagues. But that challenge inspired our leaders to rise to new levels. It made the event even more important, more prestigious.

At the time, I honestly had no idea what this event would eventually turn into. Each semester and year the presentations got better and better. I invested more time into coaching department heads on their presentations. And our department heads rose and rose and rose in their ability to present their work. This might sound a little bit silly to remember so vividly and with such admiration, but I remember the time one of our department heads got her hair done for the State of the School. This is when I realized this really was becoming an "event." You know, the kind of event that you get your hair done for.

I remember that in our fifth year of presenting the State of the School Address, we were ready to take it to another level. That's when we started doing a "run-through" two days before the event. Department heads came an hour early to work a few days before the event and practiced sharing their talks in front of the other department heads. One of our department heads was a drama specialist, so she completely understood the importance of this pre-show work - and luckily for me, she shared that sentiment with the group. Not that anyone complained. It's just that it was yet another push. It was always great to have explicit support.

One of the biggest factors I want to make sure you know about is *time*. Time is of the essence. Look, this is your big story. This is your life's work. But you need to create this presentation in a way that is in honor of your audience.

You could talk for hours about your work and your next steps, right? (If not, we have some other things we need to work on.) But the audience doesn't need or want to know your whole story. So, you need to present your story in a clear, concise, intentional, and inspirational way. Leave the audience wanting more! I usually give department heads a maximum of four minutes. Some years it was just three minutes. It pushes presenters to be concise and bring home the big points. I call the big points "mic drop moments." That's when you say something so big and important, you just drop the words and stay silent for a few seconds so the audience can take in what you're saying.

After one of the State of School Addresses at the first school I worked at, the science and history teams realized they had a shared area of work they wanted to collaborate on together. They wanted to coordinate their instructional strategies for teaching students how to make claims and support those claims with evidence and reasoning. The two departments asked to have their next collaboration day together. Science and history! Have you ever heard of such a thing?!

There can be another consequential impact of teachers hearing about the work of other departments. A team might see the awesome things other teams are doing and think, "Oh man, we are not working at that level yet." That's right. You better get on up here and get with us! Let's go!!

Let's talk about the actual event of "State of the School" itself. What does it mean to "do the State of the School Address well?" First, it takes a ton of planning. Who is doing what? How much time does each person have? What school-wide topics will we share out about (special events, special programs, attendance data, suspension data, socio-emotional survey data, etc.)? I suggest kicking off the first five to ten minutes of the meeting celebrating the many things you all should be proud of as a school. This usually includes sharing about key community partnerships, unique school programs, and overall school data (attendance, surveys, on-time, etc.). If you've got something good to share - then share it. If you don't have much to share in the area of good news, that's your current and urgent job to work on. You need to find and create good things happening at your school or district. That's part of your job, so get on it. Make good things happen. *No excuses.*

The one "given" or what I would call a "non-negotiable" is that at every State of the School Address every department head presents on behalf of their department. For elementary schools, this could be done by grade level lead teachers. For middle schools, this could be done by departments. For high schools, it could be done by pathway clusters or departments. Having teacher leaders present is the main piece that lights an enormous fire under the collective efficacy and power of the school. It breaks down the walls between departments and brings a spirit of collectivity and connectedness between the teams and their work.

You better re-read that again…I'm not even kidding. We're talking about *collectivity and connectedness,* people…And you better not miss out on that amazingly powerful combination.

Second, in order for the event to run well, department heads need support as they plan for their presentations. They need a "think partner" or two to think through which topics they are going to focus on so they can plan how to be clear, concise, and inspirational for their three to four minutes of allotted time.

As the years went on at our school, that time became more and more precious because department heads had so much they were excited to share about. That's the point you want to get to - because then you have the best of the best information being shared.

Also, if you want to put on a great State of the School Address, you also need to provide a time for department heads to practice their presentation. Trust me, presenters get exponentially better when they practice their presentations a few times through.

It's interesting: when you attend one of our State of the School Addresses, it looks like a big celebration that just…happens. I've heard of principals who tried to put on a State of the School Address and they kind-of flopped. (Boo.) There are multiple possible reasons for this. The most common reason is that the department heads weren't adequately supported or given clear enough guidelines about expectations for the presentations. An example of a misstep is a department head who drones on for ten plus minutes. Attendees and staff can get bored (people love talking about what they are excited about, but sometimes not everyone is as excited as you are about your work) and then time for the rest of the presentations can get cut short (oooh, this can make other members of your team resentful - this is not good).

So, it takes good planning and good support to put on this fabulous event.

Let's not forget the components of celebration and fun! You can put your own twist on this. The teams I've worked with have enjoyed making the event very celebratory - pom-poms, cheering for colleagues, and even dancing. With each State of the School Address, we went bigger and better. At one of the more recent State of the School events I was a part of, a team of teachers set off confetti cannons as part of the opening of the event. Imagine kicking off a staff meeting with pumping music, dancing, and confetti flying through the air - it was spectacular! Can you imagine if some of your staff meetings started like this?

An important thing to note is that there are two key types of accomplishments to celebrate at the State of the School Address: 1) hard data and 2) implementation data, which measures the implementation of strategies and practices. Hard data includes data points such as attendance rates, suspension rates, state test scores, district assessment scores, etc. Implementation data includes data points such as "eight out of eight teachers are giving a formative assessment at least twice per week and using the data from that assessment to strategically plan next steps in instruction" or "all teachers are creating one culturally responsive lesson per month which is shared with colleagues at their monthly department meeting."

I suggest you expect both of these kinds of accomplishments to be shared at the State of the School Address when possible. You will need to decide on the percentage of each based on the level of progress of your school.

For instance, during the time I was writing this book, we were planning for our first State of the School Address since the global pandemic hit, therefore, we focused the presentations mostly on the successful implementation of strategies and practices since teachers and staff had to make such monumental pivots to learn about and meet the needs required to teach through distance learning. We didn't have a ton of hard data and that was okay at the time because we were in the uncharted territory of learning to teach online. So we focused on celebrating the strategies we had been implementing and the efforts we had made and succeeded with in reaching our students, which was a truly impressive achievement at the time. Supporting the teachers and staff in acknowledging their successes at that time was absolutely critical. They had gone above and beyond to rise to the challenge of that time, so I knew we better stop and celebrate that.

We asked teachers to share their thoughts after this State of the School event - an event which was during one of the most challenging years of our careers due to the pandemic and distance learning. The presentations from our school site leaders reminded us how much we had achieved despite the incredible challenges of the time. The comments shared below show how uplifted the team felt after the State of the School event.

These were some of the comments and reflections:

"I'm so proud to be on this team! Stephens is rising up!"

"Awesome work, everyone! You are the best! Keep up the great work!"

"Congratulations to all the departments. Your hard work is paving the way for the future of this school and students' lives."

"Thank you, everyone, for being an amazing team to work with!"

These are real quotes, word for word. This process is what can provide you and the staff on your team to feel this way. Even in the toughest of circumstances.

Obviously, leading and teaching during a global pandemic and distance learning is an unusual situation. So, give your team plenty of ways to be successful under the current circumstances, which in this case was looking mostly at implementation data. You need to make adjustments based on the time and the circumstances to best meet the needs of your team.

Most of the time, though, it is critical to focus also on hard data. It comes back to the department goals and how the teams are measuring their progress toward those goals. They must know and be able to articulate and consider how their team and students are doing.

There is another truly important aspect of and reason for having a State of the School Address at these two points during the year. Because it is of paramount importance to stop...yes, *stop*... for just a moment to look at how far you have come and how much you have accomplished. This is a *key* component of the State of the School Address.

In fact, it is important to build-in processes for focusing on "wins" throughout the school year to create a culture of having and building on successes. One department head at my school starts every department meeting with each teacher sharing one win they've had during the previous few weeks. During a particularly rough start of a school year, I created a shared document that I included in our staff bulletin and asked staff members to share something they were proud of. I also included a column within that document for other staff members to comment on their colleagues' wins. It turned into a beautiful love fest of colleagues cheering each other on and celebrating each other's wins - no matter how big or small. It's like the saying "What you feed will grow." What are you "feeding" in your organization?

Teachers and staff are working so hard each and every day in one of the toughest, most important jobs out there. This is the chance to pause and acknowledge some, and maybe even, all of the accomplishments. And, if you and your team of school leaders have done a good job of leading, there will be many accomplishments to celebrate. If you find yourself with a shortage of "wins," it is your job to find and create accomplishments for your team.

For instance, our most recent State of the School event was in June at the end of our first year back after distance learning. Oh man, it was the toughest year *ever*. Luckily, I work with a superstar administrator who is great at capturing our work and events and regularly posts about these on Twitter. She created seven beautiful slides about some of the many wonderful things that happened that year including our fantastic Open House - an event where we had the first chance to welcome our families back on campus since the school year had started.

At Open House we had food trucks, a bounce house, a DJ, and local vendors and a local church, who sponsored a raffle. Her slides showed our school dances, which were spectacular! We wanted to go all-out to celebrate the hard work of our students, so for the first time ever, we held the dances at night in our lunch pavilion. We had a DJ, fog machine, and disco lights. We all danced into the night - it was so special. The students said that they had the best time ever!

Her slides also showed our staff retreat from December where we strengthened our bonds through community building activities and teachers had time to work together to collaborate. We also saw pictures of our morning of "Bagels with the Boss" and our staff luncheon during staff appreciation week. We were reminded of our professional development session for staff who were new to our school and our community building day just before school began.

The point is that we could have completely forgotten about these wonderful events. In fact, many of us had. The year had been so difficult, but these slides reminded us of the many great things we did and achieved. We had done great things. We demonstrated how we are capable of great things, even during difficult times.

One district administrator said to me at the end of one of our inspiring mid-year State of the School Addresses, "Your teachers are going to teach their hearts out today." That's it, that's the sweet spot of the feeling people should have after watching and being a part of a State of the School Address. *The future should feel like ours for the taking.*

Because it will be.

State of the School Way of Thinking

A few years ago, I was in a district professional development meeting for administrators and our Deputy Superintendent told us about a greeting used in the Masai tribe in Africa. This tribe is known for its fierce warriors and strength. As members of this tribe greet one another, they say, "Kasserian Ingera." It means, "How are the children?" The traditional response is, "All the children are well," which generally means "Life is good."

This tribe, while known for its power, has a belief about the importance of the children in their tribe embedded so deeply that it is a cornerstone of the way they communicate with one another.

What if you asked yourself each day, "How are the children?" Could that help you to stay even more centered in your work?

Some of the thinking about the State of the School comes from that same notion: How are the children? We need to be honest and heartfelt in not only asking that question, but also in answering it. Can we say with the utmost confidence, "All the children are well?" Probably not.

That is not to bring us down or to bring us any sense of hopelessness. In fact, it's quite the opposite. It means that we've got to get to work! What can we do today to take us even closer to the promised land of being able to say with a fully confident heart "All the children are well?" I want for us all to be able to say that one day - sooner rather than later.

You see...I told you that this process and way of thinking is ambitious.

Be warned, though, this process is made of powerful stuff because it works. It can be addictive. And it takes a *ton* of work, time, energy, courage, and dedication. But it is also a very strategic use of all of your resources. It is not for the weak of heart, either. You need to be ready to be your school's best leader, not necessarily their "favorite" one. You will need to be the kind of leader who not only leads with empathy and heart, but also the kind of leader who is strong and fearless enough to ask tough questions and have hard conversations.

I think of my job in the way that I think about the work of a personal trainer. A personal trainer's job is to push you to get stronger even when it's hard. If he or she just lets you do the number of push-ups and sit-ups you are "comfortable with," you will probably not reach your greatest potential. You have access to a variety of resources you can use to build and implement a fitness plan, but for most of us, we need someone to push us and hold us accountable. We need someone to know we are even more capable than we might think we are.

Your job as a leader is to push. Push with support, resources, and love. I try to pair the asking for something with the giving of something. For instance, if I expect a team to collaborate and build collective efficacy, I must also strategize a way to give that team the time and resources in order to meet that challenge. For example, I expect our department teams to collaborate, therefore I find funding for and provide paid structured days of collaboration for every department throughout the school year. If you want great work from your team, you need to give them the resources.

I observed a department meeting last week that completely blew my mind. Teacher leaders are in a tough position - they are expected to lead and push their colleagues. They need to lead and push in a way that gets their teachers on board without getting to the point of the teachers saying something like, "Who do you think you are asking us to do these things? You are just one of us." Yeah, you really don't ever want it to get to that point.

Anyway, I had a coaching session with this department head a week prior to this department meeting and I felt like it was time for me to push him - push him to push his team. He said, "I'm going to ask the teachers if they think they can have their data ready by next Friday." I could feel it was time to drive him toward a more confident stance that would convey more urgency. "No," I said, "you are going to tell them that the data is due on Friday. The end." He pulled his head back slightly and tilted his chin. He said, "I can do that?" I said, "It's not what you *can do*, it's what you *must do*. The measuring of your goals is critical in tracking your progress. How can you do that if you don't have the data?" He was sitting up a few inches higher now. He was ready to lead - lead with conviction. This is such a small shift, but yet can have such an impact. He and I talked and planned a bit more and I felt good about where he was heading.

Then I observed the meeting. Blew. Me. Away. He crushed this meeting. His agenda was well thought out, focused, clear, and ambitious. He already had his teachers observe his class and had them give him written feedback in specific areas that the department has been working on. Then he led the team in a discussion about their progress on department goals and the upcoming dates for data collection - the *deadline* for data collection. He provided shared documents and sample lessons. And the teachers on his team shared some of their own best practices. This meeting was on point!

I met with him after the meeting and shared my exuberantly positive feedback. I was so incredibly proud of him. I had only planted some seeds with him the week before - the planning and execution was *all him.* Which was awesome because he totally got to own the success. What happened during our pre-meeting discussion is that he began to take ownership and agency in his role as a true leader - a leader who takes his team to new places and levels of greater achievement. During our conversation after the department meeting he told me, "I'm just doing what I think you expect of me." Boom. Mic drop. He absolutely made my day. Because I got to know that I had done my job as a leader, too. And all I really did was say, "Here's the bar - go!" And he jumped so far above it all on his own.

As you're reading this, you might be thinking: Ah, good for that guy. He did good work that day. Yes, and it is so much more than that. First, he was modeling excellence. When he raises the bar for himself, it has the potential to be contagious. Second, he was expecting excellence from his colleagues. Which means he's raising the bar for them, too. You can probably guess where this is heading, right? You know who also gets so positively impacted? The students!! They are now working with a collaborative team of teachers with a laser-like focus on meaningful goals - and the collection, monitoring, and analyzing of those goals. Long story short, excellence begets excellence. This is the kind of thinking it takes to lead to the state of the school you are striving toward.

What is the state of the school?

How do we know?

And what do we do now?

State of the School Way of Working

Thinking about this department head who was so successful with his meeting…How did the process help to support him in his leadership and his team in their excellence?

The team started the school year with focused, measurable, and meaningful goals. The department head attended monthly leadership team meetings to support him with his thinking and planning. The department head was also held accountable for progress toward the goals during the leadership team meetings and me as the principal. I invested time in this leader by meeting with him to discuss his plans for next steps with his department and pushed him through coaching.

This department head said something very telling during the meeting with his department. He said, "I need this data by Friday because we've got the State of the School Address in two weeks and I need to present this data."

The State of the School process brings a greater sense of urgency and accountability to the work. You aren't just working your way through the book or content. You aren't just making it through until June. You are striving purposefully. All year long. And you are accountable to not only yourselves, but to your colleagues, students, parents, and community. You are accountable to Miguel and Hugo.

The State of the School process is about strategizing, accountability, vulnerability, risk-taking, lifting one another up, building leadership capacity, and striving for excellence.

There's a lot more to share...But, first, some questions for you to ask yourself and answer...

Leadership Questions To Consider:

1. What is your ambitious vision for your school or organization?
2. Where are you right now within the State of the School process and what are your next steps?
3. Which areas of this process might be a challenge for you and what are your ideas for finding support for tackling those challenges?
4. How are the children?

| 2 |

Chapter 2: Goal Setting and Progress Monitoring

IT ALL STARTS WITH KNOWING WHAT YOU WANT TO ACHIEVE

"Whenever you want to achieve something, keep your eyes open, concentrate and make sure you know exactly what it is you want. No one can hit their target with their eyes closed."
—Paulo Coelho

It all starts with goals. I cannot stress this enough. If you don't have clear, strategic, well-thought out goals, you will always be running hard but will never have a destination. Who wants to run hard with no clear destination? Not me. And I'm guessing not you, either. And I'm talking about real goals. Real destinations. Not the fake ones you write to be compliant with your boss or district.

And here's the thing - you have to not only create genuine, meaningful goals, you also have to check in on your goals regularly throughout the year. How else will you know whether or not what you are doing is working?

And your goals have to matter. They have to be real. They have to be what you really, really want to achieve.

Every business–*every business*–has clearly defined and measurable goals. So, why don't we have the same in education? Most often in business, goals are tied to financial success - and if you are not successful, your business closes. Not in education. If you are not successful in education, really, almost nothing happens. Who carries the burden of the harm of that failure? The students. Data shows that ineffective teaching can lead to the loss of two years of learning in just a single year. Two years of learning loss! That is so much lost. *Our precious students deserve better.* So much better.

And who is not carrying the true and heavy harm of that failure? Pretty much anyone who is making a salary at that school and district. Other than maybe the harm to a school's pride and joy. But at the end of the day, if a school doesn't meet its goals, there isn't a physical or financial price to pay for the people who work there. The students, families, and community bear the brunt of that burden.

Why aren't our students as important as the products we sell? How can we justify *any students* not receiving a top-notch education?

And how do we measure whether or not our students are receiving a top-notch education?

No matter what the scores are, it's likely that the same staff shows up year after year unless poor performance is handled on an individual basis. But that takes so much time and so much effort. That process is mostly for staff members that are exceptionally poor performing. People can be in education and still earn a full paycheck with a yearly raise year after year regardless of results. And most of the time, there are no incentives for excellence in education - the opposite of almost any and every business out there.

I will say, though, that I believe "above average performance" in teaching is the norm in education. There is, from what I can tell, a high percentage of teachers who are very dedicated to their craft and care deeply for their students. I believe that most teachers are hard working, dedicated, and truly want their students to achieve.

But there's still a problem, though, isn't there? Some schools are known for student success and some are not. And, if you look at trends and data in education, it's mostly the schools that serve historically marginalized populations that seem to struggle the most.

This doesn't have to be the case. I know what we have been doing at the schools I've worked with and I know that you and your school can do it, too.

We must nurture *excellence in education*. We do that by pushing for higher levels of student academic achievement paired with systems of support for teachers. We nurture excellence by expecting, supporting, and also celebrating growth.

So, let's talk about getting down to strategic hard work - Let's get down to the business of being successful in education. Because *failure is not an option - Our students are counting on us. And we are going to rise to the occasion and show up to that calling.*

First, you have to determine what you are going to measure and why you are measuring it. This is paramount. You are already going to be stretched thin. How do I know this? Because you work in education. And pretty much everyone in education is stretched thin. Therefore *you must be strategic.*

So, you have hundreds of things you can measure and ways you can measure them. How do you pick?

You need to ask yourself, "What can I measure that will truly assess my students' success?" And, "What data am I going to collect to accurately measure that?"

Some common data points to measure in education include: attendance rates, state test scores, socio-emotional survey scores, and suspension rates. You could also look at things like the tardy (or "on-time") data, the percentage of office referrals, the percentage of subgroups in accelerated courses, or scores on common grade level assessments. There are an absolute array of data points to choose from.

I like to have one or two school-wide goals per year. For instance, last year we really struggled to get students to class on time. It was very frustrating for teachers and administrators. We did the best we could with the structures we had in place, but I know that with some focused effort, we can do better. So, for this year, I will take the tardy data from last year and create a goal for students being on-time this coming year.

And on top of school-wide goals, the bulk of goal-setting happens through our department teams. Every single department sets at least two strategic and measurable goals for the year. This is where the academic work is happening, therefore this is where it must be measured and monitored. At elementary schools, goal-setting can happen through grade-level teams. At high schools, goal-setting can happen through pathway teams or departments.

There are a variety of levels at which to set academic goals and collect data for those goals. Here are a few examples:

- Individual student data
- Period data

- Teacher data (all periods)
- Grade-level data
- Course section data (accelerated, traditional, development, etc.)
- Department data

If you flinch a bit about collecting course section data, I have to tell you that one of my favorite memories as a new teacher teaching the "traditional" and "development" classes was when my students outscored the accelerated class from across the hall on the district quarter math exam. My kids were like, "What?! I'm good at math?!" YOU SURE ARE. That's what's up! Boom!

The truth is that the test was pretty darn hard and the scores were all relatively low. But my students still outscored the accelerated class.

The crazy thing is that I'm not sure my students would have ever had the opportunity to have that perspective without the district test. And, please don't be concerned about my intentions, I'm not trying to pin students against one another. But when you have a class of students, the bulk of whom think they have never been good at math their whole lives, this new perspective can be a game changer. And we wouldn't have had it without the data point of the district test.

I met with a physical education teacher once at a school I was new to - we were meeting about his department goals. He said, "I think we should have a goal for push-ups." And I said, "Why do you think you should have a goal for push-ups? Is that an excellent indicator of student achievement in your classes?" It was a real question. You see, I am not an expert in physical education, but he is. My job as a school site leader is to push his thinking - to get to the core of where he is coming from. We talked through it and we both realized that he had chosen that goal mostly because it was easy to measure.

There is no shame in that game. I get why he originally went in that direction. One critical piece of setting a goal is making sure that there are straight-forward ways of measuring them. And, frankly, he was probably not used to setting well-thought out and strategic goals that genuinely mattered. When I asked him if "arm strength" was a critical indicator of success in physical education, he paused. It seemed that no one had ever asked him a question like this about his goal before. After we did more thinking and talking, he realized that there was something even more foundational in measuring student success in physical education: cardio endurance.

So, we talked about cardio endurance and how to measure it. We came up with a focus goal, determined what data would be collected and how it would be collected. And, of course, a plan for increasing our students' cardio endurance.

What you measure is just as important, if not more important, than how you will measure it.

Another really important part of goal setting is collecting *baseline data*. You cannot determine where you are going before you figure out where you are. Let's say you decide to measure cardio endurance by tracking how much time it takes your students to run four laps on the field. The first thing you need to do is have your students run four laps around the field and time them so you get that initial baseline data. That's your starting point.

So the next thing we planned out was how to collect the baseline data so he could then work with his team to set a department goal.

The steps:

1. Determine what to measure.
2. Know why that is what you are measuring.
3. Gather baseline data to gain an understanding of where you are starting.
4. Set a goal for where you want to be.
5. Create an action plan for achieving that goal.

In math, ELA, history, and science, you could look at common grade level assessments, unit exams, formative assessments…Just know what you want your students to know and be able to do and then figure out how you are going to measure that.

Teachers need clarity on their goals to focus their work. Teachers need specific data to collect in order to be sure they are making progress on their goals. This data can also tell them if what they are doing is not working yet and gives them the signal to shift or change directions.

Our work in education matters so much - We are literally impacting people's lives. There is no time or room for guessing whether or not what we are doing is working for our students.

So, let's talk about measuring progress toward goals throughout the year. You start by setting goals at the beginning of the year and then you find ways to measure your progress toward those goals at various points throughout the year. You talk to your school-site and teacher leaders on a regular basis and you become relentless in your work together to help your school's departments and/or grade levels achieve their goals.

Sometimes I will talk to a department head about their goals a few months into the school year and they can't even remember what they are. Sometimes I have forgotten, too. This is a clear indicator that we haven't done a good enough job of monitoring our goals.

This brings us to another critical piece in the process of goal setting: progress monitoring.

Let's say your goal is to increase by five percentage points on the state test. How do you measure the progress toward that goal so you aren't waiting until June to find out whether or not what you are doing is working? You need indicators. You need to find good measurements that will inform you of your progress. And you need to look at those at regular intervals. At an absolute minimum, you should be looking at indicative data at least once about half-way through the year.

And this is when the State of the School Address comes into play in terms of goal setting and progress monitoring. It is your half-way through the school year mark. Yeah, we're not waiting until the end of the year to check in on our goals, are we? Waiting until the end of the year to look closely at data is a clever way to sort of hide under the radar, if you think about it. The whole school leaves for two months and every class of students moves on. Poof. If we don't look closely at our goals and whether or not we met them, maybe it didn't really happen. Or, "oh well, we did our best." NO. This is not good enough for our precious kids who deserve the best from us.

Miguel and Hugo are counting on you.

When you are hard pressed up against your goals *throughout the year,* you might be surprised how quickly that first half of the year goes. You have to stop and look at how you are doing in progressing toward your goals. What have you been looking at to measure your progress? This is the data you will use to report out on progress toward your goals.

Wait. Are you starting to see how powerful this can be? All departments/grade level teams stop to analyze their progress. All departments/grade level teams have to report out *to each other* on how they are doing. This creates something called "collective efficacy," which is, in essence, the power of harnessing a team's collective efforts to take the team to greater levels of success and achievement. We will be talking about this more in the next chapter.

The understanding of just how impactful this is really hit me during my second year of using this process as a principal. It was clear from the work of our school-site leaders and teacher leaders and their presentations at the State of the School Addresses that our leaders felt most accountable to *one another*. Not me. Yes, they were somewhat inspired to meet my high expectations, but it was that drive to succeed for one another that really stoked their motivation. They were mutually inspired. They saw the great work that other departments were doing and thought, "How can we be at that level of excellence, too?" "How does the level of our work and achievement align with the work of that department in order to make our efforts and success exponential like they do?"

There is a process sometimes used in education called "data chats." This is where a grade level chairperson or department head sits down with a principal and talks about department data. Sometimes this is done at the teacher level, too. These can be very impactful meetings. But here's the clincher…With the State of the School process, it's a step far beyond this. The principal will still have data meetings with teacher leaders, but the real accountability comes when school-site and teacher leaders have to report out their data to their colleagues and the *rest of the school*. And once you get even more advanced, they will report out their data and progress to the students, families, and community. With this process, the teacher leaders are not only accountable to you…*They are accountable to their colleagues.* "Peer pressure" really isn't the correct term. This is *collective efficacy*. All members of the team working together toward one goal - student achievement. And all accountable to our students and to one another to make that happen.

It's beautiful. Because it's not about the power dynamic. It's not about the "supervisor and employee" structure. It's about colleagues being accountable to colleagues. And at the end of the day, it is about us being accountable to our students, their families, and our community.

"Here's what I'm doing to support our students. And I can't wait to hear more about what you are doing." Boom.

There is another group beyond teachers, teacher leaders, and departments that must be included in setting and monitoring their goals - and I bet you already know who I am talking about...the students. Yes, them, too!

You need everybody on board when you are daring greatly! Who better to help you to achieve your goals than the students? Shouldn't they have their own goals, too? Of course they should! This is all for them in the end, isn't it?

At the first school I led, the year we started to genuinely involve the students in their tracking and monitoring of achievement data was the year things really started to take off in terms of success. Students became empowered by understanding their own data. They used their data to set personal goals for assessments and they became partners in the journey of education.

There are a variety of ways in which you can attack this. At that time, students had hard copy folders of their personal data tracking in math and ELA. Now it seems like the time for students to have electronic data portfolios as long as there is access to the technology required to do that.

A few years ago, our history department created an electronic form for students to track their progress on writing persuasive essays with a color-coded rubric for students to monitor their own progress. As the year went on, students were eventually asked to self-grade their essays, which put them in the driver's seat in terms of being responsible for their own learning.

This is the thing...If you help people to create and own their goals, and support them in reaching their goals, you have created a system of empowerment and motivation.

Empowerment and motivation through goal setting and progress monitoring. YES. Let's do this!

Leadership Questions To Consider:

1. What are your school's indicators for success and how will you measure them?
2. Why did you choose the indicators you chose?
3. Which goals do you think will have the greatest impact on your students?
4. What system will you use to have students monitor their own data and progress toward their goals?

| 3 |

Chapter 3: Collective Efficacy

"If you want to go quickly, go alone.
If you want to go far, go together."
—African Proverb

You can't transform a school all on your own. Nobody can do that. Bummer, right? For all of you independent, hard-working, over-achievers out there…You cannot create educational magic by yourself at a school-wide level. You need others - lots of others. And that part can be scary…And exciting!

At this point in my career, there is nothing I am more proud of than the results we achieved and the thousands of lives we impacted at the schools I have worked at. And I have no illusion that what we achieved was due solely to my leadership. Oh no, that was not the case. At all.

I did steer the ship. I did nurture shared leadership. I did plan strategically and I did push my team. But our teachers are the ones on the front lines who really made the magic happen. In particular, it was the leadership team - made up of department heads for each department - that fully embraced their roles as school-wide leaders. And a leader for every grade level.

None of what we achieved could have happened without them. And that is collective efficacy.

"Together teachers can achieve more, especially if they collectively believe that they can do so." (John Hattie, *Visible Learning*)

Hattie's research shows that *collective efficacy has the greatest impact on student achievement - above all other things.*

ALL. OTHER. THINGS.

I hope you are listening...

Collective efficacy has the greatest impact on student achievement above all other things including being more impactful than providing feedback to teachers; the effectiveness of classroom management, homework, and testing; and EVERYTHING ELSE.

Collective efficacy is number one.

It makes sense, though, if you think about it. People working collectively to make things happen. As one of my amazing colleagues says, "Teamwork makes the dream work."

Remember when you read about the science department and the history department who ended up collaborating on best instructional practices? Two completely different content areas, but they saw an area in which they could work together. Together they created a process that students used to create successful claims with evidence and reasoning in both science and in history. *That* is collective efficacy.

Let me give you another example. In middle schools, we have something called "grade level meetings." Traditionally, this is where grade level teachers get together and talk about students who are challenged behaviorally and/or academically and discuss plans for helping the students. These meetings were very frustrating for me when I was a teacher. For one, some of the students we were discussing were not even in any of my classes, so I got up early for a 7:30 am meeting to talk about students who I don't even know or work with. Ugh.

The other challenge I experienced with grade level meetings was that the students that multiple teachers had a "problem with," I didn't share the same concern. Me, at the meeting, "Oh, they are great in my class." (Crickets.) I don't think almost anyone wanted to hear that.

Grade-level meetings have always felt like a mixed bag to me because of those experiences. Then, over the past few years, I have seen how the idea of grade level meetings could transform - and it was only because of the stellar leaders that I worked with and the collective efficacy they created together to transform the purpose and outcomes of these meetings.

As the time approached to plan for these upcoming grade level meetings, I worked with my administrative team leaders and asked: "What do you think your grade level needs right now in terms of direction and support?" At the middle school level at my previous and current school, we have one identified leader per grade level.

I was excited about this direction because it felt like we were differentiating based on the needs of the specific group rather than what felt like complaining about students for an hour straight at one of our precious weekly morning meetings. Each grade-level leader at the time developed and implemented a plan based on the needs of the teachers and students at their grade level. The meetings included support with both instructional and behavior support practices. There was time built-in for supporting students who teachers shared, but it was done in a way that was strategically planned so that no teacher was sitting there without a clear purpose. These meetings were proactive and meaningful. These meetings were...Beautiful. The planning for these meetings was outside of the box and I loved that.

Take this to a point a few years later as we were dealing with teaching, leading, and grading during a global pandemic. This time was so rough on all of us - on absolutely everyone in the system: administrators, office staff, custodians, cafeteria workers, instructional aides, recreation aides, students, parents/guardians, the community...You name the group and I can assure you they were struggling.

These circumstances created the urgent need for genuine teamwork and collaboration. This past year, I saw our grade-level leaders lead in a way I had never seen before. We would brainstorm a theme or goal for an upcoming grade-level meeting, such as reducing the number of students receiving an "F." The grade-level leads would then create a template of information to be shared during the grade level meeting - data, insights, important points regarding context (which at that time included the challenges of distance learning during the pandemic), and ideas for empowering our teachers. After that, each leader would put their own "spin" on the meeting based on their leadership style and the needs of their team.

For instance, one leader used the story of "Les Miserables" to inspire his team. Another leader used funny memes to inject some humor into the work of the team being asked to take on this big challenge. Another leader used inspirational quotes and videos. They all had the same message and were inspired and pushed by one another as they shared their Google slides into the late hours of the evening before the meeting to be held the next morning.

What was special was that the work was so incredibly aligned to the work of the entire school, yet delivered in a unique way based on the individual leader and the group they were working with. The talk and work done across the campus for the following weeks was highly focused on the ability of teachers to impact student success in terms of grades - and this had a big impact on improving the percentage of students who were able to pass their classes, even under very difficult circumstances. This wouldn't have happened without the collective efficacy of the team of grade-level leaders.

Another example of collective efficacy is in the way we use our "adjunct duty hours." Adjunct duty hours in the district I work in are part of the contract. Adjunct duty consists of twenty hours outside of the regular school day per semester to support the school and students. When I first started as a teacher, I was asked to sign up to support a number of school events as part of my adjunct duty hours. I supervised dances, helped to plan for a school fair, and supported supervision efforts at bus duty after school.

This is, as far as I know, a very common approach to fulfilling adjunct duty hours in my district. A year or two into my principalship, I realized I could utilize these precious teacher-hours in a much more strategic and impactful way. I developed something I called "Adjunct Duty Teams." These teams would focus on areas essential to our school improvement including: attendance, growth mindset, Young Black Scholars (focused on the academic and social emotional success of our Black students), awards and celebrations, and school operations. Teachers then chose which team they wanted to work on, which is an essential piece of the equation. I find that people feel the most empowered when they have a choice.

We had the first Adjunct Duty Team meeting during a staff meeting so that teams could meet, establish goals, and decide on the best time and days for future meetings. After that, they would meet about once a month and then carry out tasks in support of their goals.

As I write it, I marvel at how simple it sounds. It's so simple, yet it can be so powerful.

These teams drove the work in each of these areas and it made a substantial impact. I know this because they had the data to show it! Because, of course, the leaders of these teams also presented at each State of the School. Through the work of the attendance team, attendance went up! Through the work of the Young Black Scholars team, our Black students showed incredible academic gains and also scored higher in their "sense of belonging" in our social-emotional surveys. Our students' ability to feel a strong growth mindset also improved as shown by survey results.

It wasn't always a perfect upward trajectory. But the fact that we were closely monitoring this data throughout the year gave us insight into the work we were doing and the progress we were making. We started to find out what worked and what didn't work based on the data. We were operating within a system of continuous improvement - and through this system, we made consistent and substantial gains over time. It works. For real.

I would be remiss if I didn't add that there was a process for accountability, which in most cases, in my experience, is a strong driver for good and equitable work.

The process of accountability shouldn't feel cumbersome or condescending. I had a shared drive with folders for each Adjunct Duty Team. In the folder was a simple template for the team's goals, a list of the team members, and then a running sheet of tables where the team leader could input team meeting dates, members in attendance, tasks, and hours contributed.

It isn't a perfect system because I'm sure some team members still contributed more than others, but it can be a way to at least encourage all team members to make a contribution. Every few weeks I would review each of the folders and would make note of contributions and progress. If I noticed a team member wasn't listed for multiple meetings, I would reach out to the team leader to discuss the situation and see if that person needed my support.

The key to this is you start to see how powerful it is to put a group of people together and task them with something ambitious and meaningful. Especially when they get to decide on an area of work that inspires them and that is in their wheelhouse. And then they get to share about their work, learnings, data, and next steps in front of the whole staff. People...Are you hearing me?! This is the stuff that magic is made of.

Okay, another example of collective efficacy: it's something I call "back-to-back department meetings." This idea was born out of...I guess, just seeing where the core of the work needs to be done at the secondary level: within departments. I think this applies to all levels of education - in elementary schools, it would be by grade levels or similar grade levels. In secondary, it can be by departments. Content specific work is so critical. That's why I double-up on the content-specific work.

Here's an example of how a back-to-back department meeting structure can be used. In my current school, we have a school-wide focus of providing students with lessons that are culturally responsive. I am not an expert in creating culturally responsive lessons - At the time we started this process, I'm not sure any of the people on our staff were experts in this area.

So, I figured we could put our heads together and try to figure this out as a team. There seems to be something sort of humane and vulnerable in saying to a team you are leading: "I don't really know the answer…But I bet if we work together, we can figure some of this out."

Win-learn.

I said that and I meant it.

It's one of the best sayings I've ever heard. I read it somewhere and I have been changed forever since. You have two options: one is to win and the other is to learn. There is absolutely no "losing." Not in a place where continuous improvement is the culture and the norm.

As a staff, we brainstormed ways in which a lesson could be made as relevant as possible to our students. Then we tasked teachers with writing a first try at a culturally responsive lesson.

Y'all…Teachers can be incredibly creative when they are unleashed to be innovative and put themselves in the learners' shoes. This group of teachers came up with all kinds of ideas on how to create lessons that were culturally responsive. For example, two history teachers created a lesson where students did a scavenger hunt around the campus to engage thinking about the history of the school. A math teacher created a lesson about finding the area of a circle by using the radius of a local restaurant to a cross section of streets that most students were highly familiar with. The English language arts team developed a lesson where students used key literary terms to highlight lyrics in their favorite songs.

Phew. It's such good stuff.

So, we rolled with this process the whole year in what I call "back-to-back department meetings." For the first five rounds, I asked teachers to come to the first department meeting with a culturally responsive lesson plan they developed on their own while using a simple template I created.

My goal was to encourage individual thinking. These are sharply intelligent and creative teachers - I wanted to give them room to think on their own and then bring a variety of ideas to the table. And that's what they did.

At the front end of the back-to-back department meetings, teachers each brought their lesson plans with a copy for each member of their department. They would each talk through their lesson plan and explain why they chose this standard to focus on, how their plan was culturally responsive, and what independent task they were going to ask students to do at the end of the lesson to prove their learning.

Then they had the week to give their lesson and collect student work and data on the lesson, which they would share at the second of the back-to-back meetings.

Teachers would share student work and the data they collected from their lesson, which is such a powerful tool because that means they had a culminating task for students to do independently in which teachers could analyze to see if students actually learned what they intended for them to learn.

1. Share the lesson with colleagues.
2. Administer the lesson to the students.
3. Share results of the lessons, examples of student work, reflections, and next steps.

We got to round five and one of the teachers shared: "Creating these lessons on my own is wearing me out. I'm exhausted." She was not alone in this sentiment. So for the next two rounds, the final two sets of back-to-back department meetings of the school year, I asked teachers to work collaboratively in the first meeting to create lessons (rather than expecting them to bring the lessons already completed) - either create common lessons among common classes or work together to bounce ideas around to create lessons. Then each teacher gave the lesson and came back together to discuss the results, reflections, and next steps.

I've mentioned this before, but it bears repeating. It is critical to listen to the people you are working with and to make adjustments based on their needs. Assume the best intentions as often as you can. Rigidity can be the death of adaptability and creativity. I heard my teachers' concerns and I changed the process accordingly. And they thrived because of it.

I try to get around to as many department meetings as I can on the mornings we have department meetings. What I saw and heard over these nine months as teachers pushed themselves and each other to create powerful and engaging lessons was truly inspiring. Teachers' lessons got better and better, their confidence grew, and the students' behavior in class improved, as well as their academic skills, over this time.

This process is fire, people. We've done it seven times this year and it is done with every single teacher in every single department. Every. Single. Department. PE, math, history, special education, science, health, electives, English language arts...You name it, our teachers do it. Our music teacher, who is the only person teaching music at our school site, visits with a variety of departments to share the culturally responsive lessons he's created and to listen to others about what they've created.

Ideas shared tend to create more ideas. It can be the bustling creative buzz that is created among people with a shared vision and purpose. That is collective efficacy.

It also could be helpful to talk about a "non-example," as we say in education. What does collective efficacy not look like? Here is a classic example: You have three teachers working in the same department. At least one or two of them come in early and stay late doing their planning and grading. They are working so hard and they're each getting "okay" to good results. At their department meetings that happen once or twice a month, they each spend time talking about operational work, receiving "information" from their department head, and complaining about their students who are the most challenged in behavior. Then they talk about their plans for how they will decorate their rooms for Back to School Night.

This is a glaring missed opportunity. And you might be surprised to know how often it happens. Maybe you're not. You've got bright, hard-working teachers. Why aren't they using their collective brain power and energy to plan lessons together? Why aren't they creating common assessments based on the grade level standards and then analyzing and sharing the data from those assessments...*Together*? Isn't that where the *real work* is?

Using precious time together in the most effective way is critical to the success of a team. What is the "big" work - the work that impacts the most important thing: student success - and what can we do together to best tackle it?

The big work is the hard work. The big work is looking closely and strategically at your practices - in this case, let's say it's instruction. If you have teachers who are not talking consistently about instruction and working together to develop the best ways to meet the variety of needs of their students, then they are not doing the big work. And neither are you.

The "little work" is about the things we have to do, but don't necessarily lead to exponential growth and achievement. I once observed a leadership team meeting at a school where they spent a solid 20+ minutes discussing whether or not spirit wear could be part of the weekly uniform. They talked about the colors of the spirit wear and the clubs the shirts and sweatshirts represented…and…oh my God!! We were in a room of school site leaders and this is what they were spending their precious time and energy on?

So, let's talk about some potential challenges. Let's say on a team at your school you have two bright, hard-working teachers and one who has a bit less to contribute. Even though there are only two teachers ready to roll and try new things, this team still needs to be focusing on and doing the "big work." Why? Because that teacher who isn't performing as well may start to not only learn to understand the standards better by working with knowledgeable colleagues, he or she might also be lucky enough to have some of that inspiration and dedication rub off when he or she sees how much the other two teachers care, how hard they work, and the results they get because of it.

We cannot let teams fall down to the level of the lowest performing member. We must empower teams instead to lift those teachers up. I worry about how sometimes some teachers get left behind as others strive for excellence. It is a tough and unfortunately not uncommon scenario.

Right now I'm working with a history department with three teachers. One of them is what you might call "old school," in that she is very traditional in her approach to teaching. She cares about her students and is trying her best. She has made great gains in the area of using technology in her classroom, which to me, was a signal that she is probably open to other new things, like more current and relevant instructional practices and approaches to history content.

This teacher works with two powerhouse teachers. In terms of history teachers, they are the most "cutting edge" history teachers I've ever seen. They love to think outside of the box and are always looking for ways to teach their history content in a way that is fresh and relevant to their students, who happen to be from traditionally marginalized populations. These two teachers make history come alive and they are doing some really cool stuff.

One of their recent lessons was on "power and perspective." They had the students not only think about who had power in the past, but who has power in the present - and how those two things are connected. They even retitled their class, calling it "Voices of America - Immigrants, Women, and the Forgotten" while using the most modern literature in history to study history. It is amazing to see people working at this level of creativity, dedication, and impact.

The department head, one of the powerhouse teachers, and I have been working together to figure out strategic ways to bring our more traditional teacher into the fold of this culturally responsive and engaging work. I asked him how he could be more inclusive with her. It reminds me of the African proverb, "If you want to go fast, go alone. If you want to go far, go together."

It has been tricky for this team to align because due to their different instructional approaches, they are in completely different parts of the book within the first month of school. And, if you're sitting there wondering why I would be okay with that, I will be the first to tell you that I will take creativity in pacing while also meeting the standards any day over going chapter to chapter through a book. Own it, be passionate about it! And then teach the heck out of it.

So where could this team possibly start in terms of aligning in a meaningful way? The powerhouse teachers came up with a plan. Since one of their department goals was to help students to improve their persuasive writing, they decided to have four writing assessments throughout the year. These writing assignments were outside of the usual history content, but the topics were connected.

Except for the very first writing assignment, in which they used a "hook" approach to get students to think and write. The first writing assignment was on whether or not pineapple should be a pizza topping.

So no matter where each of the three teachers were in the book, they all stopped to teach this persuasive writing lesson. They worked together to come up with the idea, to investigate relevant articles for students to use as resources, and even wrote the lesson together about how to teach students how to approach this writing assignment. And they do these common writing lessons and assessments four times a year. This has given them the chance to plan together, critically think together, analyze data together, and not only self-reflect on the lessons and data, but also offer peer feedback to one another.

Of course, the students began writing about content-specific history and the teachers strategically planned instruction built in to increase their students' confidence over time. And the students crushed it. They became more and more proficient about evaluating sources, stating a belief, and then supporting it with solid evidence.

This is a life skill. And this, my friends, is evidence of collective efficacy.

You see, this is an example of a way to embed some collective work and build your capacity as a team. It doesn't have to be "all or nothing," though, "all" is the highest level of collective efficacy. Trust me, some collective efficacy is better than none. A lot of it is even better. And you will be amazed at the organic changes that come about as teachers and school leaders become more accustomed to and effective at working together collaboratively. The key is to start.

Speaking of starting, collective efficacy can happen in so many ways throughout the day. It can be planned or it can be spontaneous. I'm going to put this in writing and I hope it doesn't offend, but you cannot have collective efficacy if your door or your mind, for that matter, are usually closed.

Recently I had an assistant principal tell me, "I don't know how you do it, but I feel like you always find time for me - or for anyone at the school - whenever I need it and somehow you make it feel like I'm never being a bother." Yes. Of course. How could working with your teammates ever be a bother? Being as available as possible is exactly what I am going for. To be honest, the conversations and collaborating I've had with the assistant principals, school site leaders, and teachers have not only helped them and supported our school, but have helped me as a leader, too. Collaborative conversations with key leaders and teachers can bring insight, be thought-provoking, and can create new ideas for next steps. These conversations take time, love, and caring, but they are so worth it. Teachers and leaders on your campus deserve this level of time and attention - and they will thrive when you give it to them - and so will you.

Next up in the logistics of building collective efficacy is the process of empowering the teachers. First, you give them clear and attainable stretch goals so that they know what they're working toward. Then you give them the next most important thing: time. You give them time to work together and the expectation that after they work together, they will have a product. It's not time to complain about kids or work on their love lives, it's time to collaborate and produce. And that time can produce extremely valuable results if teachers are driven, focused, and use the time wisely. They can and they will if you guide them there.

So, how do you get that time for the teachers to collaborate? In the school district I work in, it currently costs about $175 to fund a substitute for the day. The hourly rate for teacher collaboration outside of the school day is, on average, about $65 per hour. Therefore, teachers can get six hours of collaboration at less than half the cost of paying them outside of the school day. Plus, I find that teachers are exhausted after teaching all day, therefore this gives them the chance to come in "fresh" for a full day of collaboration with their colleagues. It is worth the time, money, and time away from the classroom. Trust me. And, this is coming from someone who is almost obsessive about teachers having as much face-to-face time as possible with students. So, I do not make this recommendation lightly or without a tremendous amount of contemplation.

Can you imagine the power, results, and growth that could come from working together like this? Where can you start strategically aligning collective efficacy at your school, department, or district?

I've never seen anything more conducive to building collective efficacy at a school site than using the State of the School as a way of thinking, as a process, and as an event. The State of the School can turn a spark of collective efficacy into a raging inferno of powerful force toward shared achievements and success.

Leadership Questions to Consider:

1. What structures do you currently have in place to create opportunities for collective efficacy?
2. What structures will you add in order to create more opportunities for collective efficacy?

| 4 |

Chapter 4: Shared Leadership and Building Leadership Capacity

SCHOOL TRANSFORMATION REQUIRES A TEAM OF LEADERS

"Talent wins games, but teamwork wins championships."
—Michael Jordan

As the principal, I know we need an abundance of leaders on campus for a variety of reasons, but one main reason is that as an individual, I have only so much time and energy. I can't be everywhere at once. I need groups of leaders to lead their teams. It sounds so simple, doesn't it? But, honestly, are you doing enough to nurture the abilities of your school-wide leaders? At elementary schools, this could be grade-level leaders or leaders of K-2 and 3-5 cohorts. In secondary, you could have department heads, professional learning cohort leads, or pathway coordinators. The point is that you have a smaller team you lead and nurture in terms of its leadership capacity in order to have these leaders go out and lead their teams.

The power of this philosophy and practice is truly astounding. Nurture, inspire, and empower your school-site leaders. Work with them to create a vision. Put them in charge! Yes, *put them in charge*. It doesn't have to be all you. In fact, it *can't* be all you. You can't do it all anyway. Sorry for having to keep reminding you of that - I know it might be disappointing to hear that. But there's good news, too. It's going to be even more fun and even more rewarding...And even more successful when you share the leadership. *Achieving the results we have achieved as a team at my previous school and current school has been so much more exciting and rewarding than any individual accomplishment I have ever had.* Because you get to look into the eyes of your teammates and colleagues as the amazing results come in and get celebrated and you get to say, "*We* did that." We. Did. That.

It is *the best feeling*.

How can you, as a leader, support this spirit of connectivity and collaboration?

Something I have learned during my years in education is that people need and deserve to have "think partners." Someone to work through the thinking behind an idea. That's what I consider to be one of my main roles as a principal. If you are a school-site leader or the leader of a team, this is an absolutely critical part of your work. If you are a department head or grade-level representative or a leader of anyone or any group of people, I am talking to *you*. If you are leading or supporting in any kind of a way, be "that person" for your colleagues to help them to set their sites high and create a strategic plan to reach those goals.

Sitting down with someone who is leading a team is so beneficial for so many reasons. For one thing, it signifies an investment in someone's work. It conveys a clear message about caring about what someone is passionate about - this message is invaluable. One of the most precious things you can offer to someone is your time and attention. It is not easy to fit this time into your schedule (trust me, I know), but it is important enough to make the time to do so.

Second, you need your school-site leaders to truly lead if you want your school to be successful. Never, never forget this. You need a multitude of leaders across your campus or organization to fulfill the vision you have. You cannot do this alone. How do you show how much you value someone? You spend time with that person. You ask him or her what he or she thinks. You work through challenges together.

So, *talk to your leaders. Push their thinking. Lean on their expertise.* And work together to create a plan for success. It is honestly one of the most empowering things you can do as a leader.

I had a teacher tell me once that she has seen and talked to me more times in just the few months of working with me than she has seen or talked to any other principal *in her entire career.*

WHAT??!!

Here's the thing, team. You have got to make time to meet face-to-face with your people. You cannot transform a school by yourself. You are going to need a team. So, if you don't already have a strong team - you better build one. Quick. And do you know how you build a team? *By talking to them.*

And what's the first thing to talk to them about? Them.

Them.

And then you ask them about their *goals* and *vision* for their work. They have been dying for someone to talk to about this.

Educators, in my experience, get into education because they care. They care about kids. And they care about our future. Sometimes people can get caught up in the grind of work. And that is pretty natural because work in education can be quite a grind. Your job is to help your team to remember "the why" - why they got into education, why they want to work hard to make a difference, and why they have been given this moment, this opportunity to make a difference, to impact their students' lives.

So, let's talk about logistics. As a principal, I would argue that the two most important meetings of the month you are in charge of include your staff meeting and your leadership team meeting. The staff meeting is probably the most obvious in terms of importance because that is where you work on school-wide efforts and set the tone for your culture and climate. But the leadership team meeting is where so much of the magic happens. It's where you empower and then deploy your school-site leaders.

In so many educational systems, there is the principal at the top and then, other than an assistant principal, a flat bar of the next level: everyone else. No, no, no. First of all, I like to think of my assistant principal as the co-principal. Boom. That way you are already sharing your role at "the top." There is plenty of work and accountability for everyone, so stop hogging it all. Then there is a whole new level next: the school-site leaders. You can't just use that term as if it's in theory, you have to mean it. I invest in and trust my department heads just as the army's sergeant trusts her corporals.

Let's talk about a couple of examples of ways to share leadership and build the capacity of your leaders.

I'm sure you walk through classrooms, right? To observe instruction, learn more about what's going on at the "ground level," and to provide feedback to teachers. A great way to utilize this practice you're already doing in an even more strategic way is to bring your school-site leaders - including department heads or grade-level leads - with you on these walkthroughs.

Right out of the gate after hearing that, I can feel some of you getting that nervous look on your face. The elephant in the room is the question of: Have you created a culture where it is safe and supportive enough with a dose of the ability to take risks at your school to the point where teachers will welcome other teachers into their room?

It's a valid question. You're a smart person. I know this because you've invested your time in reading a book to give you ideas on how to be better at your job.

What do you think you could do to create a culture where teachers welcome other teachers into their room? Here are a few ideas: encourage risk-taking and model that yourself; explain to teachers that you are excited to see all the great things going on in their classrooms; consistently talk about your work in terms of continuous improvement in order to build that mindset; and give all teachers the opportunity and means to visit other teachers' classrooms in order for them to learn from one another.

I've found that a big part of how well an idea is received is dependent on how it is framed or messaged. How you say it, as in how you sell the idea, is just as important as the idea itself. Don't worry...There's more on this later in the book.

Once you have a culture of improvement, it is time to walk through classrooms with your school-site leaders. How could you possibly expect them to lead if they don't have a clear picture of what is happening in the classrooms of the teachers they are leading?

As you visit classrooms with your leaders, ask them about patterns they are seeing. What things are going well? What evidence did you see of the implementation of school-wide practices and expectations? What ideas are emerging in your mind in terms of next steps for the work of your team?

Not only does this practice enhance and build the leadership capacity of your teacher leaders, you might even learn some things by hearing their thoughts and perspectives on what they observed during the classroom visits. They might notice things you don't. They might have grade-level or content-area expertise you can learn from. Be willing to be vulnerable enough to learn from the people you are leading - it can be a treasure trove. And at the same time the teacher leaders can be learning from you, too, and your expertise in seeing things from a big picture perspective. I've found that teacher leaders are grateful for the opportunity to work with you in this way. Working with your teacher leaders in this way can help them feel more valued and have a strong sense of partnership in the work.

This is building leadership capacity and sharing leadership.

Another area in which you can share leadership with your team is in the area of accountability and the use of data to drive the work of a team or department. I have a process for having teachers submit formative assessment data via a shared folder on our Google drive. Teachers from each department submit their data, reflections, and next steps on a template in a folder that is specifically for their department. About a month into using this new process, one of the department heads asked, "When do the teachers need to submit their data to you?" And I said, "It's not due to me…It's due to *you*."

The teachers in each department were accumulating data on both individual and shared lessons. People who should really be looking at that data, other than me, are the department heads. That way the department heads can look for patterns in the data and determine if there is work they will need to do in department meetings to address anything that arises in the data.

For instance, the math team might see that 6th grade students are struggling with the standard of finding the discount and mark-ups of items. The department head could provide ten minutes of work time in the upcoming department meeting for the 6th grade math teachers to discuss the data and come up with a new plan. She might even have the whole team listen in and give ideas or suggestions.

Another possibility is the department head will notice one teacher's students have significantly more success with a formative assessment for a certain standard, so the department head could have that teacher share her strategies for teaching that standard. Woot woot! So powerful.

In December after the Thanksgiving break at my new school, I was preparing to roll out a critical school-wide effort around formative assessments. I felt very passionately about this effort and was excited and nervous to roll it out. At my previous school, I had made the pitch for regular, common formative assessments at a staff meeting and at that time, I had already been the principal there for four years, so the staff trusted me and jumped on board.

At this point in the year at the school I was working at, we didn't have another staff meeting until January and the pressure to start this school-wide practice was pressing on me. I had to roll it out at a leadership team meeting and get them to sell the idea to their department teams. It was the perfect opportunity to empower them as leaders. It was an exercise in trust...And faith, to be honest. So, it was the day before the meeting and I had a pain in my stomach so bad, I could barely walk. It was bad. I had everything ready for the leadership team meeting the next day. I limped out to my car at the end of the day and hoped I would be in less pain the next day.

I wasn't in less pain the next day. I was in more pain. I was up at the ungodly hour of 4am and I knew I couldn't get to work that day. I started figuring out a plan to have someone else lead the meeting. After about 10 minutes of plotting, I realized this meeting was just too important to miss. I used the early morning hours to get ready as gently as I could. I hobbled into work slumped over with every step. But I made it. And I gave it my absolute all at that meeting. Because working with the leadership team is sacred. I could not miss it. After the meeting, I headed to urgent care and was diagnosed with diverticulitis.

I'm not telling you to put yourself in harm's way in order to lead a meeting, but I do want you to understand how important it was to me to be at work that morning. I would have missed most any other day under the circumstances, but not this time with the leadership team. These meetings are too important and our work is too urgent. This is your sacred time to build the collective efficacy of your staff.

The great news is that the teacher leaders were on board with the plan to implement common formative assessments after our meeting. I knew the idea would be best coming from the teacher leaders. I had heard the teachers had been quite resistant to other school-wide initiatives in prior years, so I knew I not only had to show up, I had to knock it out of the park.

And this is where we come back time and again to the importance of helping people to understand the "why" of what you are asking them to do. Without a clear understanding of the "why," teachers can feel like they're being asked to implement "just one more thing" that will "go away" as has happened so many times in the past. If you've got a great idea, you have to SELL IT. You thought you were in the field of education, didn't you? No, my friend, you are in the business of sales. More on this later.

Another very important aspect of the leadership team meetings is that teacher leaders will get their guidance on what to do during their department meetings. I have seen and heard of the absolute worst waste-of-time department meetings. You know about them, too. It's where the department head or grade-level lead shares some sort of operational information such as when the new workbooks are coming in and the times for the upcoming Back to School Night. Then teachers can spend the rest of the meeting complaining about their students. Oh my...What a waste of time and what a disempowering meeting!

Our weekly meetings run every Thursday from 7:45-8:45am. My goal is for teachers to feel more motivated, inspired, and equipped to kick butt every Thursday morning by 8:45am. And the way to do that is to use that time putting their big, fabulous brains together to plan lessons, analyze lesson plans, analyze student work, analyze assessment data, talk about and learn best instructional practices...Anything but the kind of operational stuff that can easily be handled in an email.

Yeah, I said it. Handle that operational stuff in an email. "But what if teachers don't read their emails?" OK, well, what are *you* going to do about that? Do you have shared expectations about how often teachers are expected to read their emails? Do you talk to them about it when they are clearly not reading your emails? Do you explain how you are using weekly meetings for more complex work, therefore operational information will be disseminated via email? Make it work, people. Stop making space for excuses and wasted time. You can do hard things!

Collective efficacy is about using time together wisely and strategically. Get everyone working together and you will not believe what can happen! It will be hard work, but they will love it. Do you know why? Because they are going to start to rely on one another, learn from one another, use their time more strategically at meetings and in their classroom.. and then they are going to start to see *results*. And it's going to feel awesome.

Leadership Questions to Consider:

1. What will you do to build the capacity of your school-site leaders?
2. What opportunities can you add in order to create a space for greater shared leadership?
3. Is there anything you need to do to work on the culture of your school in order to create more space for excellence?

| 5 |

Chapter 5: Vulnerability and Risk-taking

IF YOU WANT NEW RESULTS, YOU HAVE TO TRY NEW THINGS

"Our deepest fear is not that we are inadequate. Our deepest fear is that we are powerful beyond measure."
—**Marianne Williamson**

A critical element in implementing the State of the School process is to support teachers in a way that allows them to be vulnerable enough to take risks. I would even argue that a school-site leader probably cannot achieve maximum results without having a staff that is willing to be vulnerable and take risks.

There can be a tendency in education to do things "the way they've always been done." This tendency certainly will not create an environment of change and growth. Doing things the way they've always been done will leave you stuck with the same results as you've always had. I'm always surprised when teachers analyze their results and are disappointed with them, but don't have any plans to do anything differently.

You know what this is all about, right? It's about blaming the kids. Or blaming the parents. Or blaming the community or the district or the…You get the idea. I often wonder if we try to blame everything else so that we don't have to do the hard and scary work of looking at our part in our students' success…Or lack of it.

Why should we be vulnerable and take risks? Because growth doesn't happen unless you push yourself outside of your comfort zone. Also, taking risks can help you build your confidence.

I believe almost all of us are only scratching the surface of our potential. And part of the reason for that is we are somewhat predisposed to stay in our comfort zone. It's the big "what if?" What if I try and fail? What if I embarrass myself? What if I stretch too far? But *what if you don't?* What if you try and *succeed?* What if you find out you are capable of achieving so much more? What if you find out you can impact hundreds, maybe even thousands of lives?

Do you really know for sure what is possible? Wait…I want you to really think about that for a minute. What do you think is actually possible if you stretch the limits of your current perceptions? Just take yourself one step beyond what you currently believe is possible. What is there? What do you see? What is possible?

It's a super scary thought, I know. To realize you are capable of so much.

In order to be transformative, the school staff needs to take charge of things they are in control of. For instance, we really can't always control parents, or community violence, or poverty…But we can control how we teach and how we strategize. But before that, we need to commit to being vulnerable and taking risks.

There are a variety of ways teachers will need to take risks. One way is that teachers will need to look at their students' academic success data - and, maybe even just as importantly, look at it alongside their colleagues so they can work as a team to reflect and address gaps in learning and instruction. This can potentially be more scary than it sounds - especially if you are willing to take a good amount of responsibility for the results. Teachers need to be able to say, "Gosh, my students really struggled with finding the main idea of the text on this assessment." Instead of saying things like, "Oh, the students always bomb that part" or "It's just too hard for our students to read this level of text." The teachers who are going to be most successful say: "What can I do better in order to help my students be more successful?"

The math team at the first school I led was composed of some of the most courageous risk-takers I've ever worked with. (The teachers at my current school are quickly getting to that level, too!) They constantly looked at data head-on, shared their missteps and learned from them. Their ability to be vulnerable and take risks in their work clearly paid off when you look at their student achievement results over the years.

I remember one teacher who came from a charter school who wasn't accustomed to being held so highly accountable for student achievement data. We met at the end of the summer to analyze the results of the state test from the previous year. He was in tears. And his kids didn't even do badly. He just saw that his students didn't do as well as other teacher's students did. This shook him to his core. To his *core*. Because, above all, he cared for his students from the depth of this soul. He wanted them to have the best of everything.

He said that day: "This will never happen again." And it never did. He had some of the highest rates of growth in our school and even in our district in the following years. He took risks, faced data head-on and learned from his colleagues. He got extremely dedicated to understanding the standards and the level of rigor the students were expected to tackle on the state test. He worked with his colleagues - they shared lessons, created common assessments, and talked openly about results. He became a fearless and indomitable expert in strategic instruction while still building strong relationships with his students along the way.

This all led to him absolutely *crushing it* with his students. I'm talking about way beyond the predicted possible results to eye-popping student academic achievement results. And, I cannot stress this enough, he did this all the while building the most solid and personal strong relationships with his students and their families. His students adored him and wanted to rise to the occasion for themselves but also they wanted so deeply to make him proud.

Another example of awesomely productive vulnerability and risk-taking within the math department is when the math department head came up with this idea called "phone in pocket." I get dizzy with excitement every time I think about it because it is so genuinely beautifully risk-taking and courageous.

The math team had been working together and practicing risk-taking on a regular basis for quite a few years before this idea came to fruition. The math department head started by trying out the new strategy first herself. The goal was for teachers to improve the kinds of questions they were asking students in order to promote students doing the thinking rather than teachers hand-holding students to find the answers. Students can be exceptionally good at "waiting the teacher out" when it comes to tough questions. Their thought process sometimes is, "If we just wait, eventually the teacher will give us the answer or at least show us how to do it." This is not our students' fault - they've been accidentally taught this behavior. And, it's not entirely our teachers' fault either. Teachers are working desperately and under a great deal of pressure to get through a ton of content and here they all are with all of the answers...It's not about having the answers, it's about giving students the power to learn. Low on time, high on stakes - It's a tough scenario.

The question of what to do when a student doesn't know the answer is essentially choosing between the easier road, which is not even that easy, versus taking the tougher road which requires the teacher taking the time and energy to make space for the hard work of expecting students to do the "heavy lifting" of problem solving and thinking. And, also, the teacher needs to get out of the way in order to make that happen. The teacher needs to resist the enticement of being the "sage on stage." The teacher needs to make room for the blossoming knowledge of his students.

In order to give students the opportunity to do the heavy lifting of deep thinking and problem solving, the teacher needs to ask the right questions that allow them to do that.

So, how do teachers get better at doing that? Especially when it requires quite a bit of "on the spot" thinking? They needed to try it, listen to themselves, and reflect in order to figure out how to do it even better next time.

The department head presented her students with a math problem and then pressed "record" on her phone. "What do you notice?" "What is the question asking you to do?" "What do you think the answer will look like?" "What do you already know that you can apply to this problem?" "Why is the y-intercept important in solving this problem?"

This strategy of asking questions in order to teach is more unusual than I wish it was. It is also incredibly powerful for students to be the ones to courageously work their way through a problem. I think back now to many, many times I should have asked my students more questions rather than just showing them how to solve a problem.

So, the department head shared this recording with her team at the next department meeting. And she fearlessly puts her work in front of her team knowing that some of her questions were good and some could have been much better. The team analyzed each question and the student responses. They gave feedback on ideas for better questioning next time. The department head listened, acknowledged, and welcomed the feedback. She said to them, "Thank you for the feedback. I can't wait to try it again and try to do even better. And now it's your turn."

She then asked all the teachers to use the "phone in pocket" during at least one of their lessons in the coming week. At the next department meeting, a week later, several teachers were willing to share their "phone in pocket" recording and get feedback from their colleagues. Every one of the teachers felt strongly that they learned a lot from this process and also made a commitment to trying to improve their use of this strategy. They even agreed to do the "phone in pocket" process again!

Powerful stuff. Vulncrability.com!

This is how you grow. *This* is how you take risks.

You might be wondering about ways in which you can model vulnerability and risk-taking as a leader. This is one of my favorite things to do. Because it reminds everyone that we are all human. And I truly believe that if you are not taking risks, you are at risk of not growing.

I had given some feedback to one of our English language arts (ELA) teachers last year and I realized that the best way to show her what I wanted was to model it for her. But, guess what? I was originally a math teacher. I'd never taught an ELA lesson in my entire life. And what I felt deep in my soul about stepping into this scenario with a distinct lack of expertise and a great sense of humility: This is a *perfect* opportunity. I loved that I had never taught an ELA lesson before. Do you understand how clearly that conveys vulnerability and risk-taking? I told her, too. I said, I'd love to model a lesson in your class, but I've never taught ELA before so let's consider this an opportunity to learn alongside one another. And, I asked her if I could please model the lesson in one of her toughest classes classroom-management-wise. If you're going to go all in, you better go *all in.*

I loved every minute of it. She told me what she wanted to teach that day and what standard she wanted covered. I used her resources and created the lessons using my strategies - the ones I was hoping to see her use more of. I said, "I honestly have no idea if this will work or not, but I'm just going to go for it, okay? Thank you for letting me learn by trying this out." I meant every word I said. For the record, being authentic and honest is one of my core values, so if I say it, I mean it. I believe it is an important way to honor and respect people. Plus, I really just don't have the time or energy to tell people untruths.

The ELA teacher who let me co-teach with her was awesome for letting me do this. She let me take the reins of her class and trusted me to do my best to teach the standard she wanted to teach. It was thrilling, humbling, and educational. Some of the things I tried totally worked and some needed some adjustments. I learned a lot. And so did the students. And so did the teacher. The teacher got to see strategies in action that I was asking her to use. What better way for her to see them? Maybe just as importantly, she got to see in action that her principal was willing to try new things and to publicly take risks in order to grow and learn. What better way to promote vulnerability and risk-taking?

And guess who else saw me taking a risk? The students! Here we are every single day asking our students to take risks in learning about new things and trying things they've never done before. I was grateful and honored to have this opportunity to show our students that I, too, was willing to take risks, try new things, and go into uncharted territories in order to learn and serve them the best that I could.

Now…let's talk about dancing and the vulnerability that comes with it.

Dancing? You probably didn't expect to be reading and thinking about dancing while reading a leadership book, did you?

During one of our State of the School Addresses, I was playing a mix of songs that I had specifically procured for the event. Fun, bright, uplifting songs. I might have done it for myself as much as I did it for anyone else. I love to use music to get "pumped up."

As people excitedly came in, the music became more and more prevalent. There's always a distinct "buzz" in the room on the morning of the State of the School Address. People are excited. It's just delicious.

It was time to start "the show." I was thinking about how to get the audiences' attention because everyone there was excitedly talking to one another and enjoying their coffee and breakfast snacks. It was like the moment when you're at the movies and the movie starts running. It's the best moment. The Black Eyed Peas chimed in.. "I gotta feelin'…"

Something in me sort of clicked. I've been dancing around on the dance floor in my living room for many, many years. But this was the first time I just couldn't contain my excitement and joy in front of our team.

"I gotta feelin'…That tonight's gonna be a good night."

It was morning. It was *early* morning. But the music just overcame me and I pumped up the volume. And then I started dancing up and down the aisle.

Eeek. Yep. That's what happened. I honestly couldn't contain myself any longer. It chokes me up to think back to this moment. It was totally unplanned. Totally spontaneous. It was pure joy bubbling up inside of me that had to be released.

I just started dancing up and down the aisle.

I felt so proud of our team and so joyful.

It felt so good.

I don't quite remember the details of what the response of the "audience" was, but I do remember that I felt and saw people getting pumped up and enjoying the moment, too.

We were in "flow." We were collectively experiencing joy. And it was a pure delight.

I have and still do feel so very vulnerable about that morning. It was so spontaneous and so heartfelt. You've already read about taking risks and being vulnerable…Well, this was it for me.

It was almost a year later that the experience really sunk in for me. I realized dancing has been a great opportunity to model risk-taking and vulnerability. So, in one of the most vulnerability-inspiring experiences I've ever had as a leader, I came as humbly and graciously as possible to our operations team, which included our administrative team, counselors, office supervisor, plant manager, and campus staff assistant, and asked them, "Next State of the School, will you dance with me?"

I don't know if they felt pressured or inspired, but they agreed to do it.

I had told the team, "If we are going to ask language learners to step into an academically content-heavy class like history and science and expect them to dive in and learn, how can we model and experience vulnerability on that level ourselves? If we are going to ask teachers to stretch themselves and try new things, how are we modeling that, too?"

I truly did and still do believe that if we expect something from someone, we should be more than willing to show that we are willing to do it ourselves, too.

So, at the next State of the School Address, our operations team led a surprise choreographed dance at the beginning of the event. By far, the most joyful part of the experience was seeing the surprise and excitement on our staff's faces. It was a sense of "Oh, hey, okay now, I guess we're working at this level.." It was pure, vulnerable, sweaty, risk-taking, joy-filled bliss.

I have heard that I have now been dubbed the "dancing principal" in our district, which makes me giggle.

Okay, so let's get something straight here. This is really important. I do not want anyone to think that they have to do some kind of a dance at the beginning of their State of the School Address. Oh, no! Not even. What I do want you to do is to find your authentic core of inspiration and figure out a way to share that part of yourself and your team with your staff.

The State of the School Address does not have to be and should not be boring. It should feel special and collective - like a group of people coming together. You know those moments in a music concert when the singer or band stops singing, holds the microphone out to the audience, and quiets down the music? The audience starts singing the lyrics, sometimes kind of quietly and hesitant at first. And then, once everyone realizes they are safe and surrounded by fellow music lovers who do, in fact, know all of the words to the song, they begin singing confidently and beautifully in harmony. It is magic. Really, pure magic.

The question is: How can you create a sense of magic for your team at the State of the School Address?

For one thing, I suggest you take your ego out of it. Focus on becoming the number one cheerleader for every single person at that school. This part really takes some vulnerability, energy, and enthusiasm - I suggest you cheer your head off as each presenter walks up and also as they walk off. *You better know* how overwhelmingly hard it is for many teachers to stand up and present in front of their colleagues. It takes tremendous risk-taking, preparation, and courage - and they will rise to the occasion to the level that you expect of them.

I remember seeing this process evolve over time at the first school I worked at. With each State of the School Address, the presenters became more and more well prepared, and brought a higher level of excellence each and every time. As you've read, we started having a run-through a day or two before the event to practice in front of one another, practice presenting efficiently within the time limit, giving each other constructive feedback and just generally making sure we were on-point. Slides started to be completed earlier and earlier and were made with more creativity, as teachers strove for higher levels of excellence. Teachers started creating pre-written speeches for their presentation. They were getting "in it to win it" by bringing their best selves to the event.

Ooh wee...I cannot even tell you the joy that brings to my heart. Watching people lift themselves up higher and higher, not only finding out what they are made of, but also being willing to share their gifts in front of their colleagues. They were also modeling vulnerability, risk-taking, and excellence.

Oh, yeah. It is a beautiful thing to watch.

I usually make an effort to buy a new dress for each State of the School event. For a few of the State of the School events at the first school I led as principal, I had a dress made for the occasion. It was my way of acknowledging the importance of my team's work. I wanted to look really nice for them because I wanted them to know how special they are to me.

At one of the State of the School Address events, I had a surprise for our attendees and staff. I had coordinated with our awesome music teacher to have a surprise show from our choir students at the very end of our presentation. She and I (and the choir students) were the only ones "in" on it. In the last few minutes of our State of the School Address, about twenty-five students suddenly shuttled into the front of the library in front of about seventy audience members. They were incredibly nervous, it was easy to tell. But I knew they were going to rise to the occasion.

Our music teacher started playing on the keyboard the first couple of notes to the song, and then the students hesitantly and a bit nervously started to sing. "You're broken down and tired...Of living life on a merry go round...And you can't find the fighter...But I see it in you so we gonna walk it out." I am tearing up right now as I write about it. The vulnerability these students were displaying just by showing up right in front of us at this early hour to sing this beautiful song by Andra Day was one of the most exciting, heart-wrenching, and inspiring moments of my career. It was like they were calling to us to call on them. "See us" and "feel us" was the message I heard. "We need you and we believe in you to take us where we need to and can go." I don't think there was a dry eye in the house.

The Assistant Superintendent came up to me after the event and said, "You know that after that experience the teachers are going to teach their hearts out today." Oh, yes, I knew. I knew.

And that's what teachers deserve. They deserve to feel inspired and uplifted. They deserve to be reminded of their "why." They need to see that we are all willing to put ourselves "out there" to take risks, to be vulnerable, to strive for excellence even when it's one of the scariest things we have ever done. How can you watch our young teenage students stand up in front of a packed library to sing their hearts out and not be inspired to take risks and rise to excellence too?

Be vulnerable. Take risks. Strive for excellence. Show up, even when it's the hardest, hardest thing you'll ever do.

Everyone is watching. Everyone is learning by what you say and do. Speak your words and walk your talk. And model that we are going to put it all on the line because our work is *that* important.

Leadership Questions to Consider:

1. How can you, as the leader, model vulnerability and risk-taking?
2. How will you show your staff that you support a culture of risk-taking?

| 6 |

Chapter 6: Keeping the "Why" at the Center of Your Work

WHAT IS YOUR "WHY?"

"Once you clarify your purpose for doing something, the way to do it becomes clear." —Oprah Winfrey

This work is everything if you understand the "why" of you showing up to it day after day despite the struggles and the challenges. This work is almost nothing without the "why." If you don't have a strong, deep sense of why you are in education, I humbly and strongly suggest that you search elsewhere for your true passion.

I believe every person has been given and/or developed amazing gifts they are obligated to share with the world. A dear friend of mine named it beautifully as your "sacred obligation." What you were put on this earth to do.

Yep, I know. It's pretty deep and pretty heavy, but there you go. It's the truth.

What is your sacred obligation? You need to know the answer to this question. I want you to know what your sacred obligation is so you can share your gift with the world. You have unique gifts - you were put here on this earth at this moment for a reason. What is it?

If you can't identify your unique gifts and your sacred obligation, please stop reading, stop everything, and contemplate this. Go into the quiet. Get into nature. Dance around your living room. Do whatever it takes to make some space for this question.

You can even ask your inner circle to name three things they think you are best at. I can already tell you about at least one of your unique gifts and that is you are a dedicated learner. I know this because you are reading this book right now. Look at you go investing in your personal and professional growth! I see you and I celebrate you!

I was once an event coordinator before entering into the field of education full-time. Event coordinating is hard work, but it was also "sexy" work because it was so dang cool. I loved it. It was fast-paced, intense, and exciting. It definitely met several of the criteria of what I was looking for in terms of my life's work.

What I mean by "sexy" is that there can be perks - fancy events to attend and famous people to meet, if you work for the kind of companies that do that sort of thing. And you can get paid a very good salary. You get sneak peeks into events and openings that few others get. You meet people who have access to limos that get you to concerts with VIP access and seating. That is sexy work, if you ask me. I know because I've had and done all of that in my days as an event coordinator.

Then, when 9/11 happened and the bulk of events in the United States were canceled, I got a chance to work in education again. That's when I started the long term substitute assignment that changed my trajectory. That job in education changed my life forever.

After teaching that class from November to June, I was hooked for life. There was nothing I wanted to do more because I found a job in which I *made a difference.* I made a difference in people's lives. What could be more rewarding?

You can also make a difference and impact people's lives as an event coordinator. It's not about which job makes the biggest "difference," it's about which job you were put on this earth to do in order to leave *your* mark.

When I started teaching, I was in hook, line, and sinker. I kicked my leg out of bed every morning because I knew my work impacted people's lives. It was an addictive feeling. Even though it was so hard. I knew Miguel needed me. I knew Rayquan needed me. I knew Hugo needed me. It was beautiful. I loved showing up for them everyday. And I loved it more than working tirelessly to try to make sure that we could provide an not-to-be-named actress from the early 90's with extra limos in order to bring her friends with her to a big celebrity event. Though, someone has to do that job!

Mind you, the night in the VIP section at the Elton John/Billy Joel concert will never be forgotten. RIP sexy job and sexy perks.

All joking aside, education is where I found my true calling. I believe my divine purpose is to help people find their true potential, which is very, very oftentimes completely beyond what they initially imagine. That is my favorite part, too. People seeing in themselves a new version of what is truly possible.

An amazing way to more deeply understand the power of knowing your "why" is to watch Simon Sinek's TED talk on "How Great Leaders Inspire Action." It's incredible. It made my brain explode because it just made so much sense.

In the talk, Sinek discusses the importance of not only knowing your "why," but also the importance of effectively communicating it. He explains that the "what" is what you have to offer, what you are selling. The "how" is how you provide the product or service to your client. The "why" is about why you do what you do.

Conventionally, we start with the "what" when we talk about our work.

"What do you do?" I teach math.

"How do you do that?" I study the state standards, implement the most effective teaching strategies, and collaborate consistently with my colleagues.

All good. Are you ready for it?

"Why do you do that?" Because I believe I can change the trajectory of a student's life by showing them what they are truly capable of. I can teach students to be critical thinkers. I can teach students how to advocate for themselves. I can help to empower students who have historically been marginalized to find and know their power in the world. Through this work I can impact not only a student, but a family and a community and a city and the world.

Oh, snap. That's what's up.

That's why I get out of bed each morning. And I don't just get out of bed, I jump out of bed because I know and live my "why." I know my purpose, why I was put on this earth.

And one of the only ways to get through the toughest of times, and there will likely be many, is to have a solid, fearless, relentless grasp on your "why."

What is your why?

Simon Sinek says in his TED talk, "People don't buy what you do, they buy why you do it."

Okay, I need you to sit down because I have something wild to tell you.

Okay, you're probably not reading a book standing up, so here it is...

Guess what? Yes, you are in the field of education. But you are really in the field of *sales.* Yes, you read that right. You are in the field of sales. *Sales.*

Oh no. Are you freaking out? "Wait, what? No, I'm in education. I teach. I lead."

Yeah, I know. You are 10% in education and 90% in sales.

The reason I say you are in sales is because you have to sell people on what you want them to do. If you are teaching students, you need to sell them on *why* they need to know the content you are teaching. If you are a teacher leader, you need to sell your teachers on *why* they should take risks and try new things. If you are a principal, you need to sell your teachers, your whole team, in fact, on *why* you are asking them to do what you are asking them to do.

The "why" is everything.

Too often we lead and mistakenly focus only on the "what."

"Here's what I need you to do..." I've seen and heard about it many times. No one wants to listen to what they need to do unless they also are told why they should do it. People being told what to do without the "why" leaves most of them feeling frustrated and overworked.

I don't really enjoy being told what to do. Does anyone? Unless someone clearly explains to me *why* I should do what they're asking me to do. And I'm not talking about the "You'll lose your job if you don't do this." That only fosters compliance, not buy-in. People are not inspired by compliance. I'm talking about the most respectful and meaningful way you can convey the message of getting someone to do something. This isn't to trick them - it's to take the time to explain the why. "I need you to present at the principal's meeting because your work could really inspire and help other teachers." That's pretty much all you need to say and then I'm in for whatever you need.

When I try to explain this concept to students, I tell them how my preference is to drive fast. I love driving fast. It's so much fun. And I feel like I'm a competent driver. When I think about the law, I think, they're just trying to lessen my joy by making me drive slower. But then, when I understand the reason for the law - that driving at the speed limit strongly supports your safety, the safety of your passengers, and those driving around you - *I'm in.* I'm 100% in. In fact, some people make fun of me because I drive so carefully when they are in the car. I know my "why" and my why is to keep my precious people safe.

Whenever I talk to students and parents about the rules at our school, I try to honor them by making sure I include *the reason why* we have the rules we have. For instance, we require students to wear an ID every day to school. This helps us to make sure that if something happens and we need to identify a student, we can easily do it with their ID. For instance, one time we had a student who had a seizure in the hallway during the passing period. The student wasn't able to talk at all and the administrator who came across him didn't know the student. The administrator was quickly able to identify the student from their ID. Got a call into 911 and contacted the parents. All because the student had on their ID.

We also don't allow students to wear hoods at school. This is so we can easily see who everyone is on the campus and we can get anyone's attention quickly, if we need to. You can obviously decide whatever you need to in terms of making the school rules, but I sure hope you have a reason for each and every one of them. Having rules without a reason is about power and control. Having rules with purpose is about humanity, safety, and respect.

Simon Sinek says in his TED talk, "The goal is to do business with people who believe what you believe." Anyone can do a job. But will they give their blood, sweat, and tears alongside you? That is the question. Do we believe so strongly in what we are doing, we will work outside of our comfort zone, be strategic, and actually rise above others' expectations of us? Heck yes, we will.

Simon Sinek says that when you effectively communicate the "why," you "drive behavior." When you are in sales, you need to drive behavior. How, as an educator, are you using a shared "why" to drive behavior?

I often feel like sometimes I am standing in front of my staff trying to sell them something new and there's no way they're going to buy it. I keep circling back to the why and the why and the why. And I feel like almost every time, my team has responded with, "Okay, let's do this." It's rad.

I'm telling you, again, pretty much all the people who are in the field of education because they are driven to serve, so it's important to help them to remember the reason they were driven to serve in this work in the first place. So often that sense of purpose can get lost amongst all the "have to do" lists in our work. We can get bogged down in the compliance, and the challenges, and the perceived "impossibilities."

Not if you keep your "why" at the core of your work and help others do that, too.

"The 'why' makes people want to be a part of what you do," Sinek says in his talk. Isn't that what you want? Isn't that what you dream of? For people - students, parents, teachers, staff, etc. - to be a part of what you are doing, what you are dreaming of for your school?

Let's get this. Let's get down to business. Let's do major wildly crazy awesome things. Let's let our students' and staff's lights shine brighter than even they ever thought possible.

It's deep down delicious.

Leadership Questions to Consider:

1. What is your "why?"
2. How can you share your "why" with your team?
3. How can you help to center each teacher's "why" in the work on a regular enough basis that people are grounded in that understanding as you tackle the tough challenges?

| 7 |

Chapter 7: Formative Assessments

HOW DO YOU KNOW THEY KNOW?

"Three things can not hide for long: the Moon, the Sun and the Truth." —Gautama Buddha

I don't even know how to lean into the importance of this chapter in a way that conveys its deep, deep impact on the possibilities of what you can achieve.

Every time I meet with teachers as they are sharing their lesson plans, I ask, "How do you know they know?" As in, you've taught your lesson, now how do you know the students learned what you wanted them to learn? What evidence do you have of their learning? A gut feeling doesn't count.

Almost every time I ask teachers that question, they haven't really arrived at that part of the planning. They were immersed in the planning of the instruction. Which, I totally understand. That is the bulk of the heavy lifting in instruction. I get it.

But...how do you know they know?

That is the question.

I was in a meeting with a wonderful ELA teacher and we were talking about her lesson plan for her first formal observation of the year. She walked me through all the parts of her lesson - and she did a great job in scaffolding the lesson for her students. Then I asked her, "How will you know they know what you set out to teach them? What will they do to prove it?" And, at that moment we gave birth to what we now call "Prove Its."

Hashtags were super in at the time, so we actually called them #proveits. I loved it. I loved everything about it. I still love it!

How do I know you know? You *prove it.* You prove you know.

In order for students to prove they know what you set out for them to know, you have to give them the opportunity to show they know.

Get it? Otherwise, you're kind of just guessing. "I think they know.."

How do you know they know?

Ideally, formative assessments, or "ProveIts," should be given daily at the end of each lesson. At a minimum, I would suggest they be given every other day.

This was one of those times where I presented an idea/plan to the staff and had no idea how it would be received. As you can already predict, I focused on not just the "what," but also the "why." The "what" is the "Prove It." The "why" is: You need to know whether or not students learned what you intended for them to learn today. You provided all of this great instruction…But…

How do you know they know?

This was about four years into my role as principal, so I also believe we had some trust built up by this time.

One department head was so excited about the concept she said she wanted to get a tattoo with the hashtag "Prove It" on her arm. It had transformed the way she thought and taught. It also transformed her work as a department head. She now had a clear path in which to lead her team.

What are we measuring and why are we measuring that?

What are you teaching and why are you teaching that?

And…*How do you know they know?*

Let's talk about the name "Prove It." What works so strategically is that if there is a common name, there can be an explicitly common practice. Once we rolled out the idea of "Prove Its," all teachers and students knew what they were. Students would ask at the beginning of their class, "Are we going to have a Prove It today?"

We've had many conversations around whether or not Prove Its should be graded. I lean toward the camp of letting the data drive that decision. For instance, if 90% or more of students get the Prove It correct, I will give a grade for that Prove It. If less than 90% of students get the Prove It correct, I use the data as a source of information and consider how I need to reteach the concept in order to develop a higher rate of proficiency.

That advice is not black and white and as you probably know, decisions about grading can be very personal for many teachers. I believe if 90% of my students know what I set out to teach them that day, then I believe I was mostly successful. I will also determine a way to provide extra support to the 10% of students who didn't get the problem correct. Mind you, if you have a few minutes to go over the Prove It after the answers have been submitted, most, if not all the students in the 10% category will understand their misconception in solving the problem.

The connection of this practice to the State of the School is that the data gathered from Prove Its should inform teachers of their progress toward the department goals. They are like little mini-progress check-ins. You don't want to wait to find out what your students have learned by the time they take a test or even just a quiz. As a teacher, I want to have that information well ahead of the assessment so I can make adjustments to my teaching.

Another important point is that the Prove It data - regular formative assessments - should be driving the work of all the teachers throughout the year. They can even use it as part of their State of the School data. It gets really powerful when teachers begin creating "common Prove Its." This is where teachers who teach what we call "alike classes" (such as 7th grade history) work collaboratively to develop a final question or two for a specific standard or set of standards.

Think of the level of understanding you need to have to develop a thoughtful, rigorous, standard-specific question. That part of the process alone contributes to teachers' greater understanding of the standards and therefore better instruction.

Then teachers are asking the same culminating question at the end of the lesson, which means that now they can compare results and work collaboratively to plan next steps.

This process is another way to pull teachers out of their "silos" and into the collaborative work space.

How are your teachers currently checking in on a regular basis on how students are making progress toward the standard(s) being taught? Are they doing it once a month? Once every few weeks? Once a week? Every day?

Those are important questions. I suggest there is another important question: What method are they using in order to monitor student progress?

A lot of teachers I have worked with use a written "exit ticket" in order to assess their students' learning. These wonderful teachers spend hours on reading, analyzing, and grading these exit tickets. It's actually an excellent practice in terms of assessing student learning. But, is it efficient?

So, if it's so important to monitor student progress, how can we use technology to make the process more efficient?

This comes back to the State of the School process - how are we regularly monitoring students' progress toward the standards?

Not only can we make monitoring progress toward the standards more efficient for teachers, if we use well-designed technology, we can get very quick feedback on student progress, but also, the students can get almost instant feedback on their own progress. In the next chapter, we'll be talking about utilizing students as partners in the work. This is such a great way to keep students in the loop on how they are doing in terms of meeting the goals of the lesson and the standards.

Okay, picture this: You are a twelve-year old and you are in your math class. You watch the teacher as she explains the lesson, you watch her do a few problems, then you do a few yourself. You think to yourself: I think I'm getting this. Then it's almost the end of class. Great, I'm off to English language arts, the class I really love. The bell rings. Oh, yeah, I have to do ten of these math problems tonight. Eek. I hope I will know how to do them. Whatever, we'll deal with that later tonight. Or not.

Then, picture this: You are a twelve-year old and you are in your math class. You watch the teacher as she explains the lesson, you watch her do a few problems, then you do a few yourself. You think to yourself: I think I'm getting this. Then she gives you a Google form with two math problems like the ones you've been learning about. You submit your answers. You see that you got one correct and the other one wrong. The teacher notices that quite a few students got the other one wrong. She goes over the problem and asks students to analyze their mistakes. You realize what your misstep was. Ah-ha. It's an "ah-ha" moment. "Now I get it." Then you write down your homework for the night. You feel really good about being able to do the problems correctly now.

Big, *big* difference.

It comes back to: How do you know they know? And, just as importantly: How do they know they know?

Leadership Questions to Consider:

1. What kind of data can you have teachers collect on a regular basis in terms of formative assessments?
2. What structure can you put in place to ensure the process of collecting data on formative assessments is happening?
3. How can you help your school-site leaders use formative assessment data to drive their work forward?

Chapter 8: Students as Partners and Creating a Strong Sense of Belonging and Team

UTILIZE ALL YOUR STAKEHOLDERS AS ASSETS IN THE PROCESS OF REFORM

"Teamwork is the secret that makes common people achieve uncommon results." —Ifeanyi Enoch Onuoha

What do you think of when you think of the idea of "students as partners?" I guess we should really start with this question: "Do you think of students as partners?"

The State of the School way of thinking is about figuring out how to best utilize all your resources - and one of the most underutilized resources is our students.

If you're not utilizing your students as a source of input, guidance, and leadership, you are really missing out on an incredible resource. This is another way to tap into your own vulnerability - where you openly admit to not knowing all of the answers to every question. Also, by asking students for input, you are taking big steps in helping to build a stronger sense of student agency at your school.

You must look for ways to engage your students as partners, as it is not normally the "way things are done." I know, sometimes I get nervous about giving up some control, so if you feel a little nervous in your stomach as you're reading about this, that's okay. The good news is that the benefits of giving your students a strong voice (i.e. buy-in, a sense of belonging) far outweigh the things you have to give up (i.e. power).

Let's talk about when to consider giving students a voice in matters at the school. If you think I am going to say give them a voice in absolutely *everything*, you will be relieved to hear that is not what I'm going to say. There are some "big-ticket/high-stakes" items that you will need to decide on as a leader, such as school rules around safety. And sometimes there will be items that will need to be agreed on by multiple stakeholders, such as school-wide grading policies. Whenever you are able, get input from the students. In fact, if you can find ways to get input, you can use that information as part of the decision-making process.

For instance, you can get the students' input to add to discussions about grading. You can survey students and ask them questions such as:

How much do grades motivate your efforts in class?

If you got a lower grade on a test, paper, or project, how interested would you be in an option to prove your knowledge again?

What can teachers do to motivate you to excel in academics?

While we're on the subject of getting input, let's talk for a minute about student agency. Student agency, summed up very succinctly, is about "voice and choice."

Think about when you have been a partner with someone or on a team in a great endeavor. You each probably had a voice and choice in how to achieve your goals. That can be a deeply inspirational and empowering experience for people.

Research has demonstrated overwhelmingly that students who have agency in their learning are *more motivated, experience greater satisfaction in their learning, and, consequently, are more likely to achieve academic success* (Lin-Siegler, Dweck, and Cohen 2016, 297).

An example of students having a voice is when teachers ask students for feedback on a lesson. How often do we do that? Not often enough, is my guess. Take a risk! Ask your teachers to survey their students and listen to them when they share with you about what they find out. It can be incredibly powerful.

An example of students having a choice is when we ask them about what they want. For instance, one of our awesome administrators has some incredible skills in graphic design. He designed eight different logos for our school - then we surveyed the students on their two favorite of the eight and then used those two designs to create our school spirit wear for the year.

During the first year at my most recent school, I had heard that the school had held an 8th grade activity the year before that was so poorly attended they ended up having to also invite 6th and 7th graders to the event to make up for the lack of attendance. 8th graders were upset because it was supposed to be an event just for them. But the school had already committed financially, so they had to do what they had to do. From what I was told, the students were not excited about the venue or the event, which defeated the whole purpose of a special grade-level event.

I am not without my own missteps in this area. I have been part of a team for multiple years that decided on the 8th grade activity for our students - without the input of any of the 8th graders.

This year I asked our student council team to do research on a variety of venues and activities for our 8th grade end-of-year event. They came up with a list of ten different venues and activities. I asked them to compile all the information for each option, including the costs and distance from our school so we could make an informed decision about the cost of busing and time needed to get to and from the event.

This is where that balance between input and administrative decision making takes place. I picked what I thought were the best three options based on costs and accessibility. For instance, one option cost around $100 per student - that, for me, was not an option in terms of accessibility.

After we, the administrative team, chose the three "best" options, we provided all 8th grade students with a survey to pick from the three options and had them choose in order of their preferences. You know what? We sold the maximum amount of tickets possible for the event. Because students chose what they most wanted to do - and we were able to accommodate the option they wanted most because we had offered three options we knew were doable. Win-win.

An example of when a student survey made what I consider a big impact was after the summer of 2020. We were heading back to school - virtually - due to the global pandemic. From May to July of that year we saw some of the worst instances of racial injustice we'd seen in modern history including the death of George Floyd, which many of us watched via video that shook us to the core. My theory is that because we were on "lock-down" with little to distract us, we had no choice but to look these deadly incidents in the face and were not able to look away this time.

It became a time of reckoning. We saw marches being held around the country and around the world.

It seemed odd to return back to school and not acknowledge any of it. This is a harder challenge than it might sound like. But we dove in anyway, because we felt like we could not ignore it. We really didn't know exactly how to explore these issues within a school setting. I mean, some people we knew couldn't even have civilized, productive conversations about it, so how could we even consider opening up conversations about racial justice with pre-teens and teens?

What we knew in our hearts was that it would be disrespectful to our students to not acknowledge what had happened and continued to happen. Especially since 99% of our students at the time were Black, Hispanic, Asian, or Pacific Islander. Our students were also mostly impoverished with 94% of them receiving a free or reduced lunch. The racial injustice was happening to them. And it had been happening for a long time. Now it was our obligation to open up the door to having conversations about it with them.

We realized that even though we were already having to tackle the challenges of "distance learning" (students Zooming in from home and teachers teaching online) that wasn't an excuse to ignore the clear and present danger of racism and the impact it was having on our students. We needed to work on racial justice - and that work needed to start with us. It needs to start with all of us.

We created a "Building Equity Team" that teachers and staff volunteered for. I opened the invitation to everyone at the school. Five teachers and two administrators signed up.

After we created our vision and goals, we created our first set of what we called "school-wide" lessons on social and racial justice. We went all in. I mean…*all in.* We talked about George Floyd, we talked about systemic racism. We went deep…And we went deep fast.

Some of the teachers were shocked. There was quite an upheaval. As the Building Equity team reviewed the first three lessons with the teachers, the whole presentation got derailed after we shared the second lesson. A few teachers shared their deep concerns. They said, "I don't think we are ready for this. Our students aren't ready for this." "This is too painful." "This is too dark." "What if something comes up that I don't know how to address?" Other teachers praised the teachers who had spoken up. Apparently quite a few teachers felt a strong sense of unease.

The teachers were nervous…Very nervous. And understandably so. This was some heavy lifting we were asking them to do. And we certainly weren't wading into the shallow end. We dove head first into the deep end. It seemed like it was the only way. Though, honestly, I didn't really know exactly what we were doing because I've never seen it done before.

This meeting was one of the toughest staff meetings I've ever had. I was genuinely not sure what to do. Should we abandon this work? Did we go too far? But, it was so important. It was so relevant. I couldn't just shut it down.

Some of the most common questions and concerns teachers had as we started this work was: What if I don't know the answers to their questions? What if they say something that makes me or others feel uncomfortable?

As you're probably hearing from these questions, there was a strong sense of vulnerability and even some fragility on our teachers' parts. How could they talk about something they don't have the answers to? How can they be expected to discuss these issues, when they are such tough and complicated issues to tackle? It's really, really tough.

The first thing we did was we changed the name of this work from "lessons" to "discussions." The term "lessons" implies that we have the answers, whereas the term "discussions" implies that this is something we are talking about.

Even with the name change, teachers were so nervous. Many said they believed that students weren't going to participate in the discussion because the students hadn't been very vocal since distance learning started. And, again, teachers expressed that they thought the conversations were going to be too tough.

I said, "Give the lessons the best you can when you feel up for taking a risk and giving them a try." It was really tough to dial back my strong belief that this should be happening no matter how uncomfortable it made us…But maybe I didn't do enough to prepare the staff in advance. A veteran teacher with a lot of clout said, "Okay, let's just give this a try and see how it goes."

Almost all of the teachers implemented the discussions even though it felt like a big risk and we knew we did not have all of the answers. Phew. It was such a big stretch for all of us. Especially the teachers. I so admire that they took the risk to open up these deep and difficult discussions with our students.

Most teachers said that they were surprised with how well the discussions went. A few teachers thought that the discussions didn't go too well. Some teachers weren't even sure what the students thought about having the discussions. There were lots of thoughts and worries, so guess what we did? We *asked the students* what they thought of the discussions.

We sent out a survey to all students and asked them two multiple choice questions and two open-ended questions:

Question 1: I think it is important that our school provides us with the time and space to talk about racial and social injustices (real and systemic issues happening in our world today). Rate on a scale from strongly agree to strongly disagree.

Question 2: I feel that the discussions we've had so far on race and racism have been beneficial. Rate on a scale from strongly agree to strongly disagree.

Question 3: What other feedback do you have on these lessons?

Question 4: What other topics are you interested in discussing?

347 students took the time to respond to the survey - almost half of our students. 97.2% of students said they thought it was important that we provide the time and space to have these discussions. And 93.6% said they felt the discussions so far had been beneficial.

I don't know how many middle schoolers you know or have worked with, but this data is very compelling. If middle-schoolers don't like something, it is usually very easy for them to tell you that. It's what many people find somewhat "scary" about middle-schoolers, but I actually really love it because I appreciate hearing the truth.

The cool part is that we were able to take this survey data back to the staff and say, "Wow! They want this!" It was so much better than us just making up our own opinion. Also, the students provided ideas for other topics and provided constructive feedback.

They said, "We need help with our mental health. I am under a lot of stress." "Can we have these discussions more often?" "I think that some teachers are only having these discussions because they have to."

Our students told us the truth and helped to light the way for our next steps.

This is when they became our partners in this work.

I'll reiterate this because it bears repeating: you cannot do this work alone. Cannot. No one can. You don't have all of the answers. (Gasp.) And that is okay. Use your partners, put your heads together. Be on the journey of discovery, learning, and understanding together. Ask questions. And listen. Listen hard.

And, I'm telling you...It's a million times more special sharing this work and success with a whole team of people, with an entire school. Collective efficacy leads to collective results, which leads to collective pride. We can find the answers *together*.

One of our greatest instincts as humans is the striving to belong. That doesn't mean "to fit in." It means *to belong* - to be a part of something that is greater than yourself. It is to be someone who matters. Someone who contributes. Someone who is valued. It means that you know that you are an absolutely critical piece of the puzzle. And that you are respected and listened to. Even if you are only 12 years old.

Everyone needs a sense of belonging - including staff, students, parents/guardians, and the community. Everyone has a drive for a sense that they matter. And the truth is, everyone really does matter.

So, the question is: How can you utilize students and give them a greater sense of belonging and include them as partners in the work? Students need to understand that they are critical to the equation. Because they are! And they need to know that.

Do you know how I know that everyone matters and that we must utilize the assets of all our stakeholders, including our students? Because in my ten years as a principal, I see that almost all the data improves in unison. As student achievement rises, the percentage of D's and F's decreases. As a sense of belonging increases, so do the students' and staff's sense of safety. And that just can't happen unless everyone is working together. Everything ties together. How can you achieve that without having all stakeholders on board?

Oh man, it's time to talk about a tough truth. You may not get everyone on board (*eek*). You already knew that, didn't you? So, let me clarify that when I say "everyone" I am referring to what Malcolm Gladwell calls "the tipping point." It means that most people are on board. People who are not "on board" are considered "outliers." They are sometimes the people who are saying, "This is too hard." or "This can't work." or "Students can't do this."

The key is in understanding that these people are outliers. If you're an outlier, you're probably not reading this book. People who want to strive for higher levels of achievement and excellence are the ones who read books on new ideas on how to achieve more. These are the people who are striving for excellence, the people who persevere. The people you want on your team. That, my friend, is *you*. (Woohoo! High-five, you!)

So, how do you get people on board and give them a sense of belonging? One of the most important things to do to help to achieve that is to ask your people (staff, students, parents/guardians, the community) what they think - ask them for their advice and opinions. Sometimes I wish I was better at this than I am. But I know that the many times I have genuinely reached out for feedback and input, it has helped to lead me in the right direction.

Asking for feedback can be done in a variety of ways. One of the most common and explicit ways to ask for feedback is to give surveys. I love this way of collecting feedback and data. It's usually quite easy to implement and can give you quick results.

While I love surveys, I want to point out that it doesn't have to always be this formal. Collecting feedback can be done informally and I believe it can and should be done almost every chance you can get. For instance, I'll ask students at lunch, "How is everything going at school for you? What can we do better?" I'll also ask them, "Tell me about a teacher you love learning from this year." One of my favorite things to do is to tell that teacher that the student talked about how much he likes her class and appreciates her teaching. It always makes the teacher's day! And it is real because it comes straight from the mouths of our kiddos.

This past year I finally did something I always wanted to do, but hadn't yet made the time for: I developed a student advisory group. With the help of a teacher who had a strong sense of students who would be good representatives on this committee and who were also willing to come to school early once a month, he made recommendations about which students to invite. I was new to the school and needed his advice. I met with each student he recommended and explained the purpose of the group. The students seemed excited to "have a voice." Not only to have a voice, but to be listened to.

I learned things from this group of students that I would have *never* known or even imagined without their feedback. An example of this is that when I got to my new school, I heard feedback from the lunch staff that the lunch lines were chaotic and frustrating for both staff and students. I love a good operational challenge - these are great things to take on first thing when starting at a new school. I created a new, highly structured system for students entering the cafeteria and picking up their lunches. At first this new system made people pretty mad. Staff and students. You know, like, "who does this new principal think she is?" mad. I didn't really mind because I knew this new system was better and more efficient. There was less drama and more organization. I kept trying to reassure myself that change is sometimes hard for people even when the change is good.

So, the system continued, even got better, and more tightened-up over time. This happened very quickly, too, as in a just a few weeks. I never heard much about it again...Until I was in a meeting with my advisory committee of students.

In December, over three months into the school year, I asked my advisory team: "What is the biggest improvement you've seen so far this year at our school?" Their answers floored me. Four out of the five students said, "The improvement in the lunch lines."

I was shocked. Completely shocked.

I asked them, "How has the new lunch line system impacted you?" They said, "There is less cutting and the lines go faster." I said, "Are you sure this is the biggest improvement at our school this year?" They said, "Yes, absolutely yes."

The other student said he felt that the biggest improvement was that now students were able to use their cell phones at lunch. Cell phones...At lunch!! Surely the others would change their answer. Nope. They stood firm. The improvement in the lunch lines.

They said it so whole-heartedly that I asked them to present this information at the next State of the School Address.

Who would have known? Not me, I'll tell you that much.

Sometimes you think you know, but you might not. Ask them. Ask the students. Ask the teachers. Ask the staff. They can come with a wealth of information and insight.

There is oftentimes a focus on doing things better, which is good and courageous work. But please remember to also ask what is going right, too. You need to know what to keep doing - and you might just be surprised about what that is.

Students as partners. Ready, set, go!

Leadership Questions to Consider:

1. What questions do you need to ask your students in order to help guide your work?
2. What assets do your students bring to the table that you can harness in your work?
3. How can you engage your students in the work of school improvement?
4. What processes can you put in place to get student input? (I.e. online surveys, one-on-one or small group interviews)

| 9 |

Chapter 9: Grading

FAILURE IS NOT AN OPTION

"Failure is not an option when success is your destination."
—Unknown

Everyone...Please take a deep, deep breath. We are going to talk a bit about grading.

Ohhh my...I often say that talking about grading is as deeply personal as talking about religion or politics. When I say it's personal, I mean, in my experience of working with teachers...It is *personal*.

I can take a gander about why it is so personal for teachers, but that would require the creation of multiple chapters and potentially other books. Can we just agree that grading is quite personal? And, what I hope to show is that maybe there are some ways to think a little more "flexibly" about grading.

Gulp.

Are you still there?

So…grading…

I feel like everything I'm about to write right now could be pulled apart, dissected, and misinterpreted. So, I'm going to just put some thoughts out here and hope you and/or others you share these thoughts and ideas with might just open up a little space in your/their heart and mind for consideration.

One thing I want to start with is the idea that grades can be motivating and they can be defeating. I contend that grades are more than just a reflection of how well or not a student has met the grade level standards. Now, that. That there is controversial. And I am open to the possibility that my ideas about this will likely continue to evolve over time. I just think there is some potentially rigid thinking around grading based on mastery of the standards. There. I said it.

So, what are grades for? That is a multi-million dollar question. And this question impacts millions of people.

Grades are subjective. All teachers I have ever known or worked with have a different grading scale, different things they grade, and different ways they grade.

Let's think for a minute about grading in math. Math seems like it's super easy to grade because the answer is just right or wrong, correct? Imagine a Kindergartner who is asked to find the sum of two pumpkins plus two pumpkins. The Kindergartner circles two sets of two pumpkins together to make four pumpkins then writes the number "5." Is he wrong? Or is he half right? I believe that he is half right for knowing that he is putting the pumpkins together and deserves some credit for that. At least half credit, maybe even more.

I think about the student who gets a score of three out of five for that question because he got the concept correct, but wrote the wrong number. That student might think to himself, "I knew to put them together, but I counted wrong. I need to be more careful about counting and writing the right number. I need to remember that four pumpkins means the number 'four.'"

The student who gets a giant "zero" for her answer to that question might think, "Yep. I knew it. I suck at math."

That moment. Those moments. All of these moments. They happen again and again over time. And then you meet the adult who says, "I'm just not good at math." And I say, "No, you're probably good at math, you just didn't have a good math teacher."

Or, I could also say, "You were working within a system of grading that was pretty rigid and it gave you the misguided impression that you aren't good at math."

Which brings me to my next point. I'm going to need you to take a really deep breath for this next part..

I am wondering where the responsibility should land if students aren't mastering the content at the speed in which we expect them to. Is it the kid's fault? The parents' fault? Our society's fault? Our educational system's fault? The teacher's fault? The school's fault? The principal's fault?

The answer is "yes."

But here's the thing...There is only one person who is specifically saddled up with that failing grade. That "F" is next to the name of the class with only one person's name on the report card: that student's name.

I'm just not sure that is completely fair.

But I'm also not entirely sure about what to do about it.

What I do believe is we really owe it to our students to think a little more deeply about how we grade, what we grade, and why we grade. I'm asking *you* to consider if there might be a way you can use grading in a way that is more motivational than punitive.

And, if you are someone who is using a grading system or has a grading process that is more motivational than punitive, how are you sharing those ideas and that work with others?

In 2016, the leaders in our district created the opportunity to try something within our system called "scaled grading." Condensing this concept to the very basics, scaled grading helps to resolve the issue of the disproportionality of the weight of a "zero" in a student's set of grades. In the most simplest explanation: scaled grading makes grading more fair. For the doubters, they might say that scaled grading set the bar for grades lower.

Either way, the proof is in the pudding. Over the years we studied the correlation between grades and academic achievement at our school, we found that the better the students' grades, the better they did on achievement tests. That might seem kind of obvious. Was the chicken before the egg or the egg before the chicken? Did the grade lead to the achievement or did the achievement lead to the grade?

Let's revisit the idea around equity...And the "whose fault is it?" question.

One year I had two teachers teaching the same content at the same level with very close to the same amount of students. One teacher had two students with F's and the other teacher had forty-six students with F's. Problem, right? Which teacher do you want your child to have?

The truth is, both teachers were excellent. Both teachers were working really hard. And I would also argue that the students were achieving at just about the same level. Yet... two F's versus forty-six F's?

There is one key difference that I want to pull into the light. Forty-six students in that one teacher's class will open up their report card and be told that they are a failure. Forty-six students will now have an "F" on their report card, which in turn, highly impacts their GPA, and also their access to various high schools and career pathways. All just because they had a different teacher. If I could insert an emoji here, it would be the one with the wide eyes.. And maybe also the one with clenched teeth. Ugh.

Let me throw another bit of thinking your way. During the pandemic while teachers were learning to teach online while still getting evaluated, I never once gave any teacher anything less than an effective rating. Did I lower the bar? No. Did I offer even more support than usual? Yes. How can I put the teachers in a position where they are fully responsible for something they are not actually fully responsible for? Getting students to learn online while they are trying to learn at home under who knows what conditions? During a global pandemic? Come on, people.

I observed a teacher who would have received a "developing" rating in several standards. Do you know what I did? I took some part of the ownership of that. I thought: How could I better support this teacher to be more successful?

Do you know what I didn't say? "You got an 'F'!"

Do you know what I did say: How can we work together to help you to meet the effective level in all of the teaching standards? And do you know what? We did!

A practice I use to monitor grading at my school is: I ask my counselor to run a report each quarter or at least every semester on the percentage of F's in each teacher's classes. If I notice a high percentage of F's in a teacher's class, I set up a meeting with that teacher to see if we can work together in creating a plan to help his students be more academically successful.

For instance, if more than 20% of students are earning an F in one teacher's class, I will meet with that teacher. The first thing I will explain and be transparent with him or her about, is that we are meeting to discuss the high percentage of F's. I come at this conversation with a spirit of empathy and hope. I say, "Okay, here's the data, so what is the plan for helping students to be more successful in your class?"

I will also assure the teacher that I understand that she must be disappointed in the number of F's - every time I have ever had this conversation, the teacher had been feeling frustrated and disappointed with the low grades - she wanted help. The teacher will usually explain why she thinks so many of her students are failing her class. The usual challenges emerge: lack of work completion, low test scores, not turning in homework.

I ask the teacher to identify what she thinks might be the key challenge. Let's say the teacher believes that work completion is having the most negative impact on students' grades.

Then we work together to dissect the problem. I will ask, "Do you have any idea as to why students aren't completing their work?" Then we can consider the multitude of reasons that students aren't completing their work - and many times some of the reasons are in the control of the teacher.

We can discuss what kinds of work the teacher is giving and can develop a plan for the work to be broken down into smaller chunks for students to complete. We can talk about if the students are finding the classwork meaningful and engaging - and discuss ways to make it more so. We can talk about assessing if students are ready to tackle an independent assignment - are they possibly not doing the assignment because they don't know how to do it? We can talk about having private conversations with students and asking *them* why they aren't completing the work.

What is really effective about these conversations is that the teacher understands that they have some power and also responsibility in helping students be more successful.

Okay, like I said, this is a complex and layered concept that no one in their actual right mind would have the nerve to write about. But I would be remiss if I didn't bring it up, because truthfully, the culture around grading at your school and/or in your district can either be a part of propelling or derailing your efforts to bring the state of your school/district to the highest level.

Your challenge is to determine and implement many ways to inspire and motivate your staff and students! What propels them forward? What honors them and honors their efforts? What can you do to bring people up to their highest levels of excellence?

That is what I want you to do - all day, every day. For yourself, too. What propels you to your highest levels? Figure that out and nurture that like your life depends on it! I want you and your team to put your head on your pillows each night knowing that you have done everything within your power that you could do to help your students to succeed.

Leadership Questions to Consider:

1. Are you providing space, time, and support for teachers to discuss grading practices?
2. What research can you provide your teachers in order to help them to expand their views on grading?
3. Are you having courageous conversations with teachers in whose classes the students are receiving a disproportional percentage of F's?

| 10 |

Chapter 10: Surround Yourself with the Right People and Manage Your Wellness and Energy

YOU ARE WHAT YOU EAT

"Almost everything will work again if you unplug it for a few minutes, including you." —Anne Lamott

You know how the saying goes: You are what you eat? Well, I would contend that what you "eat" comes in every form of what you take in.

If you are going to be doing this incredibly challenging work, well, since you *are* doing this incredibly challenging work - I ask you to please think about who you are spending your time with and on. I know that's a somewhat deep thought, but...If you are taking all of this on, I know you probably feel responsible for helping to keep your staff's cup as full as possible in order to achieve this amazing work, so I'm wondering, how will you keep your own cup full?

Look, I'm a work in progress in this area, too - trying to find my way to a balanced and healthy life while having an incredibly demanding job. It's not easy and I'm certainly not doing it perfectly. Let's work together and support one another with some possible strategies to support our wellness.

For instance, I encourage you to please be as careful, thoughtful, and responsible as possible when you choose who to spend your time with. In some instances, you do not have a choice about who you spend your time with. That's just part of human existence. But, then there are the times in which you are able to choose.

If you spend the time needed to reflect on the kinds of people you want in your life and then make choices that support that vision, your life can change for the better. And this will enable you to be an even better leader.

I've found that with the demands of this work - leading a group of adults with varying sets of needs and complex personal characteristics - takes a very high level of time and energy. The reason it takes such a high level of time and energy is because I'm often shifting and navigating to meet the needs of each individual person or team as I encounter them throughout the day.

This is not a complaint - it is a requirement of the job. It has pushed me to understand the deep value in the rest of the time I spend outside of work. What I've learned is that a small group of dedicated and uplifting friends is better for my spirit and life experience than trying to juggle a large group of friends. I am slightly more introverted than extraverted, therefore I need to reserve all of that extraverted energy for my job. Therefore, what is left at the end of the workday or work week is quiet energy, the need for a soft landing, and the longing to connect safely with just one or two people through meaningful conversations, shared experiences, and laughter.

You might be wondering what this has to do with you. I am suggesting that you really look at whether you've got what you need in terms of relationships and support outside of work. I believe this is just as important to your success at work as the strategies and tools you use at work.

Where is your soft landing? What kinds of self care have you built into your life? Are you able to set boundaries with people at work and also outside of work? Do you have effective strategies in place for when you are feeling down? Do you have a good person or group of people who will excitedly celebrate your wins with you? And people to help you through the tough times, too?

Let's dip into the idea of "self care" for a minute. First let's talk about what self care is not: any kind of binge that provides short-term pleasure with long-term damage. For instance, a wild shopping spree where you go out and buy everything you want - way over your budget. You can get that "I've got all of this cool stuff" high, but then within just a few weeks, studies show that the physical items lose the excitement they used to bring you and all you are really left with is an outrageous credit card bill. Another example is: after a rough day deciding to eat a whole pint of ice cream. It might be comforting and delicious in the moment, but then there's the tummy ache, guilt, and scale to deal with later.

This is a pep talk I am giving to myself right now, too.

So, let's talk about some potentially more healthy forms of self care. Maybe it is getting into bed and going to sleep an hour earlier than you normally do. Some people like to get up early and meditate while their house is still quiet. Sometimes it's buying a nice candle that you light each night while you send loving thoughts out to those you care about. Maybe it is saving up for and buying a special item. Sometimes it is looking ahead and planning a weekend trip with someone who you really enjoy spending time with.

I think of self care as those water stations you find throughout running races. People run, and run, and run, and then boom - there's a nice water station with some cool water and orange slices and people cheering the runners on. These stations are spaced throughout the entire race. How have you arranged your "water stations" throughout your week, month, year, life?

Another piece of the puzzle in self support is finding at least a small handful of people you can trust at work and outside of work. This group of people is invaluable because sometimes work, life, and leadership can get very lonely. You are likely carrying lots of information and thoughts that you are not able to safely share because so much of it must be kept confidential. Who can be your very selected few who you can set down that burden with?

Finally, let's talk about the granddaddy of self-support practices: gratitude. Brene Brown says that there is no joy without gratitude. What kind of routines have you set up in your life to practice gratitude? One idea is to write a list every night of five things you are grateful for from that day. Writing it down is the best way because you can refer back to it, or you can go over the five things mentally if that is all the energy you have available. I challenge you to start at the macro level and work down to the micro level. For instance, someone you might be grateful for is "family." Yep, great start. Let's dig a little deeper. Who, in particular, in your family are you so grateful for today? Why specifically are you so grateful for that person?

As you dig deeper into the specifics of your gratitude, your gratitude can become more and more solidified in your heart and mind. Many times this leads to the wonderful feeling of, "Oh my! I am SO lucky!" I also very much like to think about the many things I am grateful for right when I wake up in the morning because I am grateful for so many things and I want to be sure that I keep those things in my heart as I start off on my day.

It's a great way to try to keep your proverbial cup as full as possible each day. Latch on to those good days, too, because sometimes that damn cup is going to get knocked over and fall all over the floor.

If you are in a leadership position in any of its forms, you are most likely a "giver." That is awesome! The world needs givers. And so does your school and your students.

So, I guess the question is: How can I hold high standards while still providing a strong level of support and be able to get home at the end of the day still in one piece?

Ah, that is a bit of a tough question. The answer, from me, is that you have to do the best you can. And, by that, I mean, that you are very much responsible for your own mental, emotional, and physical well-being. I think sometimes there is a fantasy that someone will come in and "save" us or protect us. Sometimes that fantasy can leave some of us feeling even more lost and alone.

That's why I'm encouraging you to be true to your gifts and what you strive to do to make the world a better place while also setting some healthy boundaries by taking care of the person who is doing that work…Yes, that's *you*!

Leadership Questions to Consider:

1. Who are your greatest confidants and supporters? How can you put in place a regularly scheduled time and way to spend time with them?
2. What do you need to add to your regular schedule in order to take care of yourself?

Chapter 11: State of the School Strategic Planning Calendar

LAYER IN THE WORK AND DO IT ONE STEP AT A TIME

"Leaders establish the vision for the future and set the strategy for getting there." —John P. Kotter

One way to get an overview of the process is to look at a sample calendar for the school year. Most truthfully, to implement this process with the most impact, it's best to do this continually over at least five years in order to reap the best results. But let's start by breaking it down into one year so you can get started right away and start getting some results that you can build on.

In this calendar you will see that the three pieces of the process (the school-wide event, the way of thinking, and the way of working) are all intertwined throughout the school year. If we look at the process through the perspective of a school year, hopefully you can get started in some way right away. The most important piece is just taking that first step.

State of the School Strategic Planning Calendar

AUGUST

Create or review department/grade-level specific year-long draft **goals and action plans** with the members of the leadership team (department heads/grade level representatives/etc) for the coming school year - meet with leadership team members one-on-one to talk through and strategize goals and action plans.

Finalize your plan for **professional development** based on the outcomes and data from the previous school year, school-wide goals, themes from department goals, and most recent research on instructional best practices.

Create and start a **strategic plan for professional development implementation** (including cycles of training, goal-setting, observations and feedback from admin, peer-to-peer observations, and coaching) - a plan in which teachers leave every professional development session feeling equipped for immediate implementation and a clear understanding of the purpose of the strategies (i.e. strategies they can use right away that have a positive impact on the effectiveness of their teaching).

Onboard new incoming teachers to get them up to speed on **school practices and expectations** and to provide explicit support as they join the team - connect them with a mentor on campus, if possible.

Spend time on **team building** and creating a strong **sense of community** to help teachers feel connected to not only the vision of the school, but also with one another.

Provide students with a warm and welcoming orientation/**"welcome back to school" celebration** before the first day of school to give students and their families the chance to spend time on the campus and interact with staff.

SEPTEMBER

Kick off the school year in a **fun and warm** way - for instance, have teachers line the entrance to the school and cheer as the students arrive, play upbeat music, have volunteers all over the campus to help students to find their classes.

Meet with each department head/grade level representative to **finalize year-long goals and action plans** - these plans should be based on buy-in from teachers in each department/at every grade level.

Hold the **leadership team meeting #1** - have each department head share their goals and action plans for the year, which supports accountability and collective efficacy.

Dedicate part of one staff meeting this month to have department heads/grade-level representatives **share their department goals** with the entire staff.

OCTOBER

Leadership team meeting #2 - provide professional development for school-wide initiatives and strategies for leadership.

Continue implementation of **professional development** cycles of improvement.

NOVEMBER

Leadership team meeting #3 - have department heads/grade-level representatives report to the leadership team on progress toward their team's year-long goals using interim data measures.

Continue implementation of **professional development** cycles of improvement.

DECEMBER

Leadership team meeting #4 - strategize the last push for the implementation of school-wide and department/grade-level instructional strategies and the collection of data to measure student progress before the first State of the School Address of the school year.

Continue implementation of **professional development** cycles of improvement.

JANUARY

Meet one-on-one with each department head/grade-level representative to discuss their team's progress toward their year-long goals - work with them on ideas for next steps to help push the team to greater heights.

Leadership team meeting #5 - work with leadership team members to develop their State of the School Address presentations.

State of the School Address for Semester 1 - dedicate one full staff meeting for department heads/grade-level representatives to present to the entire staff on their progress toward their goals, what they are most proud of from their work and results during the first semester, and their next steps - this event, when done well, is pretty much one of the best days of the entire school year.

FEBRUARY

Leadership team meeting #6 - provide continued professional development for leadership skills and school-wide initiatives and work with leadership team members to strategically plan out their next steps for semester two.

Continue implementation of **professional development** cycles of improvement.

MARCH

Leadership team meeting # 7 - have department heads/grade-level representatives report to the leadership team on progress toward their team's year-long goals using interim data measures.

Continue implementation of **professional development** cycles of improvement.

Craft a "**master schedule**" for the following year which puts the right people in the right places. Get teachers inspired about their teaching assignments/schedules and include them in the conversations about why you plan to put them where you are putting them.

Check your data to **look for and create a plan to address gaps in equity in the master schedule**. Do your accelerated classes reflect the demographics of the school? For instance, if you have 10% black students, there should be at least 10% black students in the accelerated classes.

APRIL

Leadership team meeting #8 - Finalize plan for school-wide state testing; Strategize the last push for the implementation of school-wide and department/grade-level instructional strategies and the collection of data to measure student progress before the second State of the School Address of the school year.

MAY

Leadership team meeting #9 - Begin drafting goals for the next school year based on data collected so far; begin creating presentations for the upcoming State of the School Address.

JUNE

State of the School Address for Semester 2 - dedicate another full staff meeting for department heads/grade-level representatives to present to the entire staff on their progress toward their goals, what they are most proud of from their work and results for the year, and their next steps for the next school year.

* * *

You might be wondering what to do if you are reading about this process when the school year is already in progress, but you still want to get started. I would suggest taking the ideas and themes from the calendar and get in where you can. For instance, if it's after the start of the year when you read this and want to get started, focus on the first semester process and do your first State of the School Address of the school year in June. Then jump in, follow the steps outlined in the calendar, and go for it during the following year.

The part of this process that really makes it work and gets the best results is when you continue to do it over time, year after year.

Leadership Questions to Consider:

1. Where can you get in right now on this process?
2. What is your first step?

| 12 |

Chapter 12: Roll Up Your Sleeves

"Do or do not. There is no try." —Yoda

I'm writing this chapter after getting a first glimpse at some climate and culture data from a survey given to students, staff, and families this year that is…well…a bit tough to take in. It's my third year as principal at my current school. The first year at my current school, our climate and culture data was stellar - positive gains all over the place. We were on the move and things were going fantastic. The survey was taken just before everything closed down due to the pandemic. Oh, how the tides they can turn.

The following year, the climate and culture scores went down, but that was to be expected under the circumstances. We were trying to implement distance learning and we all tried our best, but it was a struggle. I contend that our team of teachers and staff did a pretty incredible job of meeting the moment with dedication, persistence, and stamina under the incredibly challenging conditions.

Then, this year, we came back to a gigantic and shocking mess. I don't know what else to call it. It has been the toughest year of my entire twenty-one years in education. We were initially really pumped up to get back to in-person learning after almost a year and a half of being apart via online learning. The students and families said they were excited to be back, too.

We were highly focused on equity and inclusion as we embarked on the school year. Within the first few days of the school year starting, it was apparent we were ill-equipped for the year we were about to have. Students were not getting to class on time or sometimes at all, our student restrooms were being vandalized every day, and there was a very big and very public fight in the middle of the street in front of school just after school let out one day. It felt like chaos and it completely caught us off guard.

What happened these past few years will likely be studied for years to come. I can speak anecdotally about my experience - and I will give it to you straight and genuinely from my individual perspective.

It was clear that our students lost a lot during that year and a half. We did what we had to do at the time and made the best decisions we could with what we knew. We worked so hard to make it all work - asking teachers to teach online and students to learn via their computers while at home during a pandemic. We handed out Chromebooks and provided hotspots for students to access the internet. We bent, we pivoted, we adjusted, we learned, and we fought so hard to make it all work.

But we were in no way able to return to school post-distance learning with "business as usual" as we had hoped. Our students were not only behind academically, but, in many ways, they were behind socially and emotionally, too. In fact, it seems from what we experienced with our students, that many of them had not only lost pace, but had actually regressed socially and emotionally.

This is, I believe, no fault of our students or their families. Many parents and guardians still had to work while adolescent students were at home - some of them with three to four siblings in the same house, trying to learn via a computer screen. Some of our students had much of what they needed in terms of parent/guardian support and working online, but many of our students still felt isolated, discouraged, and uninspired by the learning environment.

Long story short, we came back to struggles we didn't see coming. Students had to re-learn how to sit in class for 50 minutes at a time for six-plus hours a day. They had to wear uniforms again. And they were asked to put away their phones (gasp!). They had to re-enter a highly structured environment after being in a less structured environment for a year and a half of their highly-formative lifespans at that point. They were being asked to regulate themselves and it was tough.

We, the teachers and staff, had to re-learn, too. I remember thinking: How does this all work again? What are all the things we need to do to manage eight-hundred and fifty students on a campus? We were wearing face masks all day and still nervous about getting sick - and nervous about possibly getting our loved ones sick - as we served on the front lines. We were working in an environment where we could only see a third of our students' faces - and they could only see a third of ours.

We returned to more trauma and challenges than we had expected. And it shows in the climate and culture survey data. And ours was some of the lowest in the district.

As I reviewed the data, I thought to myself: I think I need to resign. How could I possibly serve in this position with this kind of data?

I thought about reaching out to the members of my administrative team, about letting them know that I needed some encouragement to keep pushing forward (and by "keep pushing forward," I mean, "help me want to show back up to work on Monday"). I felt pretty icky there for a while.

But, then I realized that it isn't necessary for me to indulge in a response to this data in a way that isn't productive. My school doesn't need me to feel defeated or sad. My school needs me to get down to business.

I thought to myself: ROLL. UP. YOUR. SLEEVES. And let's get to work.

I have reminded myself that I love being an underdog. I love being underestimated. I love the idea that few people see the transformation that is coming.

Now I'm thinking about how to use this data to drive our work - how to use the data to harness our collective efficacy. And that's going to start with asking the hard questions.

I call these moments "roll up your sleeves moments." It's an opportunity to do the hard work.

My first questions about the data are: Do we have a problem or do we have a perception problem? Or do we have both?

My next questions are: How can we pull in the team to help address the concerns raised in the survey? How can we harness the team to work on the tough questions we need to address and create a plan designed to make our school work more effectively? How can we utilize our students as partners in this work?

There is a difference between excuses and context.

Trying to determine the best next steps after the past two years while using the experience as context, can help to drive our work forward. We need to ask ourselves the hard questions: Knowing what we know, what do we do now? If we want different outcomes, then what will we do differently?

You will be faced with immense challenges. You will be faced with things you do not want to face. Lean into the hard work. Lean into the hard questions. Lean into the hard conversations. Day after day after long, hard day. That's where the work is - that's where the growth is. If you do the scary and hard things, you can and will make progress.

Roll up your sleeves. You can do this.

Leadership Questions to Consider:

1. What are your current challenges and how can you use them to propel your work forward?
2. What are you most afraid of in terms of leading this work and who or what will you go to so you can overcome your fears?

| 13 |

Chapter 13: Call to Action

LET'S ROLL

"If you can dream it, you can do it." —Walt Disney

We need you! We need you to kick butt in education. It is absolutely vital to our world - to our progress - to our future. We need you to be courageous and creative and persistent. You cannot back down and you cannot make excuses. Because you were born for this moment.

We are depending on you. You have the gifts and you have what it takes to meet this moment in time.

As one of my favorite authors, Glennon Doyle says, *"Just take the first next right step."*

And then do that again. And do it again.

Some days it will be hard to look at the data. But you will look at it and do something about it anyway.

Some days you will feel a whole lot more "lose" than you will feel "win." But you will remember that it's win-learn and you will keep learning.

Some days it will be hard to have the hard conversations. But you will have them because they need to be had.

Some days you will feel like you have nothing left. But you will harness an inner strength that you never knew you had and you will continue to show up for this incredibly important work.

Some days it will be hard to get out of bed. But you will get out of bed because we need you.

I come humbly and with genuine hope that you will try some of the things I've shared in this book. I've seen these things work - and I know they can work for you, too.

So, get going. We've got work to do.

Help to Unleash the True Potential of State of the School

If *State of the School* inspired you, please write a review on Amazon. Your review will help to get the strategies in this book into the hands of more people who could really use them.

Know of someone who works in education? Give or send them a copy and help spread the power and joy that is *State of the School.*

If you are interested in ordering copies of this book for your district, cohort, school, college class, or team, please go to the *State of the School* website at www.stateoftheschool.com. You can also go to that site to sign up for the *State of the School* newsletter, which will enable you to get access to updates and other materials as they become available.

Thank you in advance for helping to get this book out there so that together we can help schools to reach their true potential!

ACKNOWLEDGMENTS

From the bottom of my heart, I want to thank the people who have made this journey and work possible. This book and my life's work would not even remotely be possible without them.

First and foremost, thank you to **Dr. Kristi Kahl** for being a mentor and friend and for being the originator of the "State of the School" idea. You are brilliant, fierce, student-centered, generous, strategic, and kind. My journey and the work we are doing in the Long Beach Unified School District would not have happened without your vision, guidance, excellence, and leadership. Thank you.

To *all* the staff at **Washington Middle School** and the students, parents, guardians, and community partners and members: I am forever indebted to you for taking me on a journey that I could not have experienced without the amazing people that you are. You led the way. You are the reason so many students have succeeded.

Washington Middle School family:
You are the State of the School.
Every single one of you.
I bow down to you in gratitude.
#nextlevel #cantstopwontstop
And don't you EVER forget it.

To my **sister and my "person," Marisa Hope Traver Eide** - who has said time and again, "Megan, you can do hard things." She takes my calls almost every morning as I drive to work while I psych up for the challenges ahead. My wish is that everyone has a person like my sister in their lives believing in them, pushing them forward, and supporting them. You are generous, kind, fierce, and loyal. I hope that I am at least half as good of a sister to you as you are to me.

To **Eric Cabacungan** - who always, always has my back. You took my calls time and again as I was writing this book when I needed support and sent me words of encouragement and clips of State of the School events to keep me inspired. You helped bring the whole book into fruition with your vision, creativity, and heart. You once told me, "Individually we are amazing. Together we are unstoppable." Watch out, world.

To **Charity Rock** - for being the ultimate leadership partner in our work at Washington. Your fierce belief in our school community, ability to inspire excellence and risk-taking, and brilliant mind made you an essential catalyst in the change we created. I am so grateful for you.

To **Torrie Baker** - for diving into the challenges in our work with courage and conviction. Your willingness to grow and learn is always an inspiration to me.

To **Adrienne Wong** - for making me feel so seen and so appreciated as a leader. You have been an ultimate friend, colleague, supporter, and cheerleader. You changed my life for the better when you walked into it. Thank you for helping my life to sparkle with your love, laughter, kindness, and friendship.

To **Darron Evans** - thank you for being such a beautiful source of peace, kindness, and wisdom. Working alongside you each day is an honor I am, and will forever be, grateful for. You are the embodiment of grace, humility, generosity, and courage.

To **Kevin Smith** - for inspiring me from the moment I met you. We were destined to work together, to put our super twin powers into action. You are the epitome of "good trouble" and you have been a fearless and relentless partner in this work and in my learning.

To **Tiffany Wile** - you are an exemplar of strength, courage, wisdom, and grace. You value loyalty and respect in a way that inspires me and also makes me feel safe. I am so grateful to have you on our team.

To **Dr. Jill Baker** - for listening so intently and giving me water and sunshine when I need it to thrive and grow as a leader. Thank you for seeing my heart and believing in me.

To **Dr. Tiffany Brown** - who checks in with relentless support and encouragement to support my dream of writing and sharing this book - and all of my dreams, in fact. Your fierce heart inspires me everyday.

To **Dr. Kelly An** - for being a consistent source of encouragement throughout the years and for giving me so many opportunities to share this work with fellow colleagues across the system.

To **Heather Bigelow** - for being a relentless supporter of our LBUSD students and supporting our State of the School Addresses so many times these past ten years.

To **Dr. Sandy Blazer, Dr. Jay Camerino, Dr. Chris Lund, Brian Moskovitz, Ruth Ashley, Becky Afghani, and David Zaid** - for the support you've provided in the many ways you have.

To **Marcus Galbreath, Dr. Dave Costa, Osvaldo Ocampo, and Dow Lawson** - it has been an honor and pleasure to work and learn with each of you. Thank you for being kind, smart, funny, inspirational, courageous, and tirelessly supportive.

To **Lorena Moreno and Eleni Makridis** - thank you for walking alongside me in my early days as a principal and for working so hard to support our staff, students, and community at Washington Middle School.

To **Janelle Harmon, Dawn Lomeli, Dr. Stacey Benuzzi, Monica Schaffer, Melanie Sanders, Suzanne Caverly, Marie Wilson, Samantha Dugan, and Uyen Nguyen** - thank you for being my soulful supporters and friends, especially during the writing of this book - I cherish and am grateful for you.

To **Lina Martinez, Amy Angel, Danielle Silva, Tanya Ennover, Sunday Vetrovec Dominguez, James Laub, Lyn Wright, Dr. Trinisha Williams, and Cheri Walker** - you have been such amazing partners in our work. None of this would have been possible without you.

To **Gloria Gilmore** and **Lourdes Perez** - for your "behind the scenes" support and encouragement, especially in those early years of my first principalship.

To **Wendy Rhinehart** - who has been my co-conspirator since our time together in our masters program. It was in our masters program that you became my trusted writing partner. You were one of the first people I entrusted to read the first draft of this book and you gave me honest and helpful feedback and cheered me on the whole way. Wendy, you are the most "ride or die" person I've ever met and I love you for that and all that you are.

To the Fancy Monday crew, **Dr. Christine Petit, Susana Sngiem, and Alma Castro** - for being a constant source of joy, play, support, growth, and friendship. I absolutely cherish each of you.

To my beautiful neighborhood crew, **Nancy Smith, Cindy Smith, and Jill Black** - for feeding me, checking in on me, and supporting me through two of the hardest years of my life. You have been tried and true friends through these 12+ years - I am grateful for you.

To my **Mom and Dad** - who taught me to be brave and resilient and to believe in myself no matter what. You instilled in me a belief that I can achieve anything I set my mind to - and that has made all the difference in the world. I hope I have made you proud.

To my **Stephens Middle School family** - we are taking our school on the "westside" to new and greater heights - and it is an absolute honor and privilege to work alongside you. Thank you to our teachers, students, and staff for co-leading this work, and for pushing yourselves beyond what you might have previously conceived as possible even under the most challenging of circumstances. We are learning and growing together and I can't wait to see what we are capable of achieving as we forge ahead. You really are the Pride of the Westside.

To **Kari Lineberger Jenkins** - for helping me with planning, proofreading, and bringing this book to life in a way that help others to grow into their pure potential. And thank you for believing deeply in and understanding the importance of this work.

To **Habitat for Humanity, E=O2, Congressman Robert Garcia, State Senator Lena Gonzalez, and the City of Long Beach** - for being such incredible school community partners.

To my whole **Long Beach Unified School District family** - you are my love. I have learned so much from you and our journey together. I cherish you from the bottom of my heart.

And finally, to **Eli Lund** - you are my muse. This book wouldn't be in existence without your positive and persistent insistence, ideas, and uplifting. You were there for me as a thought-partner in the earliest stages of the book and really helped to push the work of the book forward. You are the one who said, "You *have* to tell this story, Megan." And I believed you. So, here is the story.

ABOUT THE AUTHOR

Megan is a remarkable leader known for her ability to inspire others to reach their full potential. She is fierce, loyal, and unstoppable. With over 20 years of experience, Megan has worked with and learned from the best in the industry, and it drives her passion for helping others reach levels of achievement that they have never dreamed of.

Megan holds a Bachelor of Science in psychology, a Masters in secondary education, and a credential in education administration. She is an author, principal, educational consultant, leadership coach, adjunct college teacher, motivational speaker, podcast guest, and visionary. Additionally, Megan is a daughter, sister, aunt, dog mom, and friend.

Charming, down-to-earth, and engaging, she has a contagious laugh and makes everything and everyone around her sparkle. When you read her book or meet her, you're probably going to want to keep her in your world in some way. Her expertise in joy aligns with her belief that everyone on this earth has been blessed with unique gifts and that each person has something special to offer the world.

In the rare times she is not engaged in revolutionizing education and coaching people to their pure potential, she is traveling the world with friends or adventuring solo. Her adventurous heart has taken her to places around the world, which has expanded her horizons, developed her grit, and deepened her understanding of diversity, beauty, and interconnectedness.

Not interested in the "status quo," Megan is on this earth to change it for the better. And believes that you are, too.